James E.C. Welldon

The Hope of Immortality

An essay incorporating the lectures delivered before the University of Cambridge upon the Foundation of the Rev. John Hulse in the Michaelmas term, 1897 and the Lent term, 1898

James E.C. Welldon

The Hope of Immortality

An essay incorporating the lectures delivered before the University of Cambridge upon the Foundation of the Rev. John Hulse in the Michaelmas term, 1897 and the Lent term, 1898

ISBN/EAN: 9783337036485

Printed in Europe, USA, Canada, Australia, Japan

Cover: Foto ©ninafisch / pixelio.de

More available books at **www.hansebooks.com**

THE HOPE OF IMMORTALITY

AN ESSAY

INCORPORATING THE LECTURES
DELIVERED BEFORE THE UNIVERSITY OF CAMBRIDGE
UPON THE FOUNDATION OF THE REV. JOHN HULSE
IN THE MICHAELMAS TERM, 1897
AND THE LENT TERM, 1898

BY THE

REV. J. E. C. WELLDON

Head Master of Harrow School

LONDON
SEELEY AND CO. LIMITED
38, GREAT RUSSELL STREET
1898

PREFACE

THE circumstances in which this Essay has been written will account more or less for its character.

Some time ago the publishers invited me to write a book upon the subject of Immortality. They thought that such a book, if addressed to the intelligence and information not of theological experts especially, but of educated men and women in general, would not be without a certain value, as showing how much of all that renders human life sublime and sacred is involved in the belief that Man is an immortal being. The consciousness that I did not possess, and amidst my duties could scarcely hope to acquire, the knowledge necessary for the task so kindly laid upon me made me hesitate to undertake it; but it coincided with my own interests and studies, and with the reflexions that had long been present to my mind, and I could not resist the hope that, if I succeeded in executing it, it might do some good.

The book was considerably advanced, when I was appointed to the Hulsean Lectureship in the University of Cambridge; and it was permitted me to utilise for my Lectures some of the materials already collected for my book. In fact, the first and the three last chapters of the book contain the substance of the argument put forward in the Lectures, although a good deal that is explanatory or illustrative has been added to them; the remaining two chapters are new.

Thus the Essay is in part scholarly and in part popular; it is not altogether such as it would have been if it were designed for one class of readers only; but I trust that, with all its faults, it may be regarded as a serious contribution to theological thought upon one of the greatest of subjects.

J. E. C. WELLDON.

HARROW SCHOOL, *March*, 1898.

CONTENTS

CHAP.		PAGE
	INTRODUCTION	1
I.	NATURE OF THE BELIEF	11
II.	HISTORY OF THE BELIEF	64
III.	VALUE OF THE BELIEF	120
IV.	EVIDENCES FOR THE BELIEF. A. *External Evidences*	162
V.	EVIDENCES FOR THE BELIEF. B. *Internal Evidences*	235
VI.	THE CHRISTIAN AMPLIFICATION OF THE BELIEF	269

"Man giveth up the ghost, and where is he?"
JOB xiv. 10.

"τίς οἶδεν ἐι τὸ ζῆν μέν ἐστι κατθανεῖν
τὸ κατθανεῖν δὲ ζῆν."
EURIPIDES.

"Il importe à toute la vie de savoir si l'âme est mortelle ou immortelle."—PASCAL.

THE HOPE OF IMMORTALITY

INTRODUCTION

THE object of this Essay may be easily stated. Controversy rages, and perhaps will always rage around the evidences and probabilities of the Christian Faith. Such controversy has its own necessity, its own value and its own end.

But behind all such controversy lie those great questions without which the Christian Faith itself can hardly become a subject of discussion. The existence of God, and as its corollary the Immortality of the soul, are the postulates of all Revelation. If they are not true, neither Christianity nor any other spiritual religion can be true.

In trying to recommend the belief in Immortality by such considerations as are independent of Christianity, I hope it may be said that I am in a sense preparing the way for Christian belief.

There are many persons who are not theologians and yet have deep thoughts and feelings about religion ; they may be more or less instructed, more or less convinced ; they may wish or they may not wish to believe ; but they are ready to face the facts of human nature and life, although they set little store by authority ; and an argument conscientiously addressed to them is sure of a conscientious criticism at their hands. It is to them that I would respectfully offer this little book. I do not ask them, and indeed it would be idle to ask them, to accept what is said, because this or that thinker has said it ; but I ask them to ponder it and then to accept or reject it as they may think well. At least they will recognise in simple honesty the vast and vital importance of the doctrine for which I plead.

I plead for a belief in the soul's Immortality ; I seek no more than that. The revelations propounded to mankind have filled up (so to say) the area of the Immortal Life more or less positively, more or less piously. I do not in this essay aspire to fill it up. It is enough for my purpose if there be an Immortality within which the Providence of the Almighty may work out its inscrutable designs.

It has seemed to me as a Christian that I ought to say something as to the special light which Christianity sheds upon the truth and nature of the Immortal Life, and I have tried to say it in the last chapter. But the readers whom I have had in view are not so much Christians as those who stand, as it were, on the borderland of Christianity, and would gladly be Christians if they could. The mystery of Immortality remains and must remain. Every mystery is a great possibility. Life is tolerable if it closes in darkness, but not if it is known to close in nothingness. To do away the hope of another life is, as Goethe said, to do away all or nearly all that makes this life worth living. But every spiritual conception of life, however inadequate, is a witness to the soul's immortal being. The one enemy of religion is materialism.

I do not imagine that it is possible to prove Immortality. Divine truths may be believed, though they cannot be proved. Faith is the complement of reason, not its contradiction. Where facts and arguments are nearly balanced, it is Faith which turns the scale. I do not aspire to prove Immortality but to make it probable. In

Theology every belief is subject to difficulty; but it is often necessary to ask not only whether a belief is difficult but whether other beliefs or denials are not more difficult. For Man, as a reasonable being, placed in a world where the phenomena invite and indeed demand speculation, cannot blow hot and cold upon all opinions, cannot face both ways perpetually, cannot live out his life in a state of suspense or neutrality. He must incline to one side of things or to the other; he must hold one view to be more probable than another. If the soul is not immortal, then it perishes. But the belief that the soul perishes or that it may perish is in effect (as will presently be argued) the denial of God. For to deny or doubt a fact is not seldom to assert its opposite. Thus Agnosticism is not Atheism; but as, like Atheism, it takes no account of God in providing the motives and sanctions of morality, its practical consequence is atheistical.

The evidences of Immortality which are here offered are, I hope, such as the subject rightly allows. Two great principles—the principle of Aristotle, that every subject has its own laws and canons of evidence, and the principle of Bishop Butler, that probability is the guide of life—are the mainstays of religious thought and action. No mathematical fact is doubtful. No historical fact is certain. Yet conclusions are necessary as much in History as in Mathematics. And action follows upon probability as well as upon proof.

It must be remembered too that evidences, which may in themselves be inconclusive, gain weight by accumulation. Where a number of considerations tend towards a certain belief, the belief possesses a stronger assurance than any one or two or three of these considerations could impart to it. It is so especially in religion ; for religion, as expressing the relation of the Infinite to finite beings, transcends the limits of human reason, it does not admit of demonstrative conclusions, it must be to some extent vague, trustful, hypothetical. In religion he is wise who makes the most of such evidence as is possible and attainable. So Socrates in the *Phædo* says pathetically : "A man should persevere until he has achieved one of two things ; either he should discover or be taught the truth about these questions ; or if this be impossible, I would have him take the best and most irrefragable of human theories, and let this be the raft upon which he sails through life—not without risk, as I admit, if he cannot find some word of God which will more surely and safely carry him." [1]

It is difficult to be familiar with the history of human thought upon the primary fundamental truths of religion, and not to feel how little progress Humanity has made in all the centuries. The spiritual experiences of mankind are in the Vedas. The questionings and agonies of soul are in the book of Job. The difficulties inherent in Immortality were present to the minds of Pythagoras, Plato, Lucretius, Marcus Aurelius. The arguments for and against the Being of God Himself—the very arguments which are advanced and contested to-day—were the commonplaces of the Stoic, Epicurean and Sceptical Schools. Everywhere old ideas recur; old theories reappear. Human thought seems to move in a cycle. There is nothing new under the sun.

Yet who is there that may set a bound to the powers of the human intellect or the human spirit? What man knows not yet, and what it seems that he can never know, he may know some day. The splendid science of Astronomy stands as a warning

---

[1] Plato, *Phædo*, p. 85. The Translation is, here as elsewhere when Plato is quoted, the late Master of Balliol's. It would be dangerous, if not presumptuous, to translate after the Master.

against the prejudice that would set up, as it were, intellectual "pillars of Hercules" beyond which the inventiveness of man may not proceed. For both Socrates in ancient times and Comte in modern have disbelieved in astronomical discovery. Xenophon in the *Memorabilia* says of Socrates that he " did his utmost to discourage his pupils from studying astronomy to such an extent as to understand the heavenly bodies which did not move in the same orbit as the earth, and the planets and the stars which are not fixed stars, and from wasting their lives over questions about their distances from the earth and their orbits and the causes of them. For he saw no good (he said) in these speculations; not that he was ignorant of them, but they were calculated in his opinion to waste a man's life and to prevent his pursuing many useful studies. In fact, he was generally opposed to the investigation of the Divine method of ordering the movements of the heavenly bodies, on the ground that it was beyond the scope of human discovery, and that he did not think the gods would be pleased with a man for trying to find out what it was not their will to make plain to human intelligence."[1]

[1] *Memorabilia*, iv. 7, 5.

Still more remarkable is Comte's scepticism, as being subsequent to those astronomical calculations and conclusions which are probably the greatest triumphs of the human intellect. Yet these are his words: "Scientifically considered Astronomy can be little else than the application of mathematical truth to the phenomena of the heavenly bodies. . . . It is true that we are limited to the consideration of geometric or mechanical phenomena which have already been reduced to general and abstract theories by the preceding science. All attempts to outstep this field are necessarily as vain as they are idle, even in a problem so simple as that of temperature. Distant bodies accessible to no sense but that of vision will never admit of researches deserving to be called Positive in any other of their phenomena than Extension and Motion. So far as we are concerned, it is in these that their existence consists."[1] And these words were used within a few years of the revelations since made in Astronomy by the spectroscope.

It is evident that no position in science can be so unscientific as that of limiting the possibilities of

---

[1] *System of Positive Polity*, vol. i., Introductory Principles, chap. ii., p. 404, Bridges' Translation.

human knowledge. An inquiry into the evidences of Immortality, if it had never yet produced any result, would still be always right and always reasonable.

This essay, indeed, is not intended to be an exhaustive treatise. It is sometimes assumed that whoever deals with an important subject ought to say all that can be said about it. The result is apt to be that books are complete, but they are unreadable, and the teaching which they might give is borne down by their excessive weight of learning. I have deliberately left a good many things unsaid. After all, the object of writing is to please some one or to help some one.

Protestantism is the democracy of religion. It appeals to the people not because they are always wise or competent judges of religious any more than of political questions, but because conscience is sacred and supreme, and, where many minds are brought to bear upon a subject, the prejudices and peculiarities of individuals are corrected, and because candour is a part of religion and truth in itself is great and it prevails.

This essay is popular rather than scientific. It is intended for readers who are not specially scholars. It is for this reason that I have translated most quotations from classical or foreign authors which occur in it, and have generally, though not always, cited passages of the Bible in the Authorised Version.

I have tried to write it in a simple straightforward style. So far as was possible, I have avoided using technical terms. I have given at the foot of the pages the principal references for such quotations or allusions as are made in the text. But, upon the whole, I have avoided footnotes, as being needless and annoying disturbances of a reader's attention. No ancient classical writer used them or seemed to need them.

If at the end of this essay as at the beginning the doctrine of Immortality is felt to be involved in some uncertainty, may I say that I do not regret it? Uncertainty is the test of moral character. We are tested and approved by our attitude of belief and conduct in the presence of life's uncertainties. There is no such testing power in mathematical or scientific truth. It is moral and spiritual truth which tests a man and a nation of men. That is the reason why right belief as well as right action is presented as human duty in the Bible. And yet it is my humble prayer that the great doctrine of Immortality may through this essay be made a little clearer and dearer to some human soul.

CHAPTER I

NATURE OF THE BELIEF

In the experience of every man there is no such moment as when he looks for the first time on the face of death. He can never forget that moment nor ever live as though it had not been. He may have spent many years in the world, and the years may have been rich in interest and happiness, but at last he stands face to face with the reality which solemnises and sanctifies all things. From that time, even if he be frivolous and careless, he never wholly loses the sense of the awful vision. He knows that for him—for all his hopes, desires, ambitions, enterprises, victories—there is but one end. He is another man.

But as he looks upon the dead, when the first strong agony of bereavement begins to spend itself, the thoughts which are apt to arise in his mind will be such as these :

The thought of peacefulness.

The life that is over now was embittered perhaps by circumstances; it may have been harassed with care or stained with sin or tortured with pain; it may have been distressed, misunderstood, scorned, reprobated, condemned; but its end is peace. The beating heart is still. The lips are hushed. The eyes are closed as if in sleep. The last farewell has been spoken—or it will never be spoken. In spite of the keen inevitable regrets, when it is too late to speak the word which seems so necessary, so natural, comes the feeling that "the wicked" in death do "cease from troubling," and "the weary are at rest."

The thought of beauty too.

The beauty of death is as exquisite as it is transient. It has been portrayed in impressive language by a great poet whose thoughts were wont to play about the subject of Immortality.

> " He who hath bent him o'er the dead
> Ere the first day of death is fled
> .   .   .   .   .
> (Before decay's effacing fingers
> Have swept the lines where beauty lingers)
> And mark'd the mild angelic air,
> The rapture of repose that's there,
> The fix'd yet tender traits that streak
> The languor of the placid cheek,
> .   .   .   .   .

> Some moments, ay, one treacherous hour,
> He still might doubt the tyrant's power;
> So fair, so calm, so softly seal'd
> The first, last look by death reveal'd."[1]

But no one who has seen how the traces of bitterness, disquietude, wrath and all unlovely passion die away from the face of the dead will call his language overstrained. This beauty is itself a suggestion of Immortality.

Is it wrong to add that in the chamber of death yet another thought will occur to the watcher's heart?

It is (if I may so speak of it) *the thought of expectancy*. I do not know how to describe it, but it is there. The spectacle of death is somehow not complete in itself. It points to a past but to a future too. There is something unearthly—something prophetic—in the face of the dead. For upon it are written as by a Divine Hand the words *Mors janua vitæ*, "Death is the portal of life."

The language of religion answers to this intuition of the human heart. When it is said of the dead that "he is gone," or that "he has been called away," or that "God has taken him to Himself," there is an implied belief in an existence following upon death.

[1] Byron, *The Giaour*.

And not only so, but it is implied that that existence is stronger, better and more enduring than the life which the dead man lived before his death. In other words, it is implied that the immaterial part of him which survives and transcends death (however that part may be conceived) is superior to the material part which is soon or late dissolved and dissipated by death.

For what is the change that death makes?

The body of the dead remains as it was before; it is not less visible and tangible than it was; it preserves (for the time at least) all its members, bones, tissues, muscles, flesh and blood. Something has departed from it, something invisible and intangible, something that in the three sacred languages of men has been instinctively compared or identified with the mere breath (as the words נֶפֶשׁ πνεῦμα and *anima* serve to show), something that in its passing defies the keenest power of the microscope; and that something is the man himself. We say "he is gone;" for the soul is the man; it is not only a part and the principal part of him, but in religious phraseology it is himself.

It was not so always. In the early Greek world, where the belief in the soul was faint and shadowy, the body was the man. Thus in the beginning of Homer's *Iliad,* as is well known, the poet laments the many valiant souls of men that "divine Achilles"[1] in his wrath sent down to Hades, "but themselves" he adds, meaning their bodies, "made he to be carrion for the dogs and all the fowls of the air." What can be a greater difference between pagan and Christian thought than that to the one the body, and to the other the soul, should be the man? To speak of a city as containing so many "souls" is to use the language of Christ. For it was Christ who set His seal upon the belief, to which the pagan thought of the East had long been tending, that the soul, and not the body, is the vital and essential part of a man, and is more than equivalent to all the possessions and adornments of which human nature is capable. "What shall it profit a man if he shall gain the whole world and lose his own soul?" "What shall a man give in exchange for his soul?" Such is the soul in the Christian view, and the reason why the value of the soul is infinite is its Immortality.

But to come back to the chamber of death: as soon as it is admitted that the soul is of higher

[1] *Iliad,* I, 3-5.

dignity than the body, and that it is separated and released from the body at death, the questions arise, What becomes of the soul after death? does it survive and survive eternally? and if so, what is the nature of its novel or extended life? and how is its future conditioned by its past?

The Immortality of the soul is a doctrine standing by itself. It is independent of such theories as have been propounded, in ancient or modern times, respecting the destiny of souls after death. Immortality, apart from particular theories of its nature, is like a vast unexplored country; we know that the country exists; we touch its borders in the voyage of life; but no man has crossed these borders and recrossed them. So is it in the argument of this essay with

> "The undiscovered country from whose bourne
> No traveller returns."

That the future of the soul is veiled in darkness is an admission which all men must make. But the point upon which it is necessary to insist is that souls have a future. If the life of the soul ends in the hour of physical death, it is certain or highly probable that the discords of life cannot be harmonised. But assuming that the soul survives the death of the body, we are in possession of a truth that is invaluable. Life is then a mystery, unsolved as yet, but not insoluble. What will be God's dealing with the soul in Immortality we know not; but we know that He will deal with it in accordance with His eternal attributes of justice, compassion and love.

It is then the doctrine of Immortality, and that alone, which comes under consideration at present.

But in considering the Immortality of the soul it will be well to begin by asking what is meant by " Immortality " and what is meant by " the soul."

Immortality is a negative term. It denies something directly; it predicates something only indirectly. That is probably the reason why many thinkers who have agreed in making use of the term have not agreed upon its significance. They have believed in the Immortality of the soul, but they have not understood by " Immortality " the same thing. It will be right therefore to put aside such theories of Immortality as are contrary to the purpose of this essay.

1. And of these the first is the great doctrine which has played so strange and so strong a part in the history of human thought—the doctrine of metempsychosis or the transmigration of souls.

It has sometimes been ascribed originally to Pythagoras. But it is of higher antiquity and authority. Herodotus[1] in his account of Egypt says explicitly that the Greek writers borrowed it from the Egyptians. Certainly it lies at the root of that remarkable practice, the worship of animals, which is almost the heart of the ancient Egyptian religious system. But it is found commonly among primitive and savage peoples, though so far separated as the North American Indians, the New Zealanders, the Lapps, the Mexicans, the Zulus and the negroes of the Gold Coast. It is one of the beliefs which descended intact from Brahminism to Buddhism; nay, it was ennobled by the 550 births of the Buddha himself, and it was believed that in those births his soul passed not only into many human and animal forms but into a tree. It is a world-old notion which Western philosophers, like Pythagoras, inherited from the primitive East and scarcely made their own. Yet it has been revived even in modern times by Fourier and Fichte. It has been based partly upon Physics, partly upon Ethics. It has had strange results; for there can be little doubt that it originated the practice of abstinence from animal foods as a moral

[1] Herodotus ii. 123.

duty. Wherever it has existed it has produced a noble tenderness of man towards the lower animals. It has been thought to meet the scientific law of conservation of energy. It has been accepted by sensitive and scrupulous minds as answering to the requirements of the Divine equity. But it is essentially a philosophical doctrine, not a doctrine of religion. It is tinged with the mysticism, the speculative unreality which Oriental philosophy loves. It robs any particular life, and so life itself, of its unique dignity. It does not place the soul after death in any closer or more vital relation to its Creator. It affords no security, or no adequate security, for the final harmony between the soul and the conditions of its being. It has never been widely accepted, and it is now pretty generally rejected, in the Western world; and however great may be the historical and speculative interest attaching to it, it is not the doctrine advocated in this Essay.

Nor again is the Immortality of the soul as here considered anything but a personal, individual Immortality.

II. There may no doubt be an Immortality which is not individual or in which individuality is submerged. The absorption of the individual soul after death in the Universal Soul of which it is an emanation is a belief which, if not primarily religious, is yet not alien from religion. It is ancient, as all ideas respecting the soul seem to be ancient. It was the teaching of Anaxagoras among Greek philosophers. The Greek and Roman poets not seldom make allusion to it, although somewhat obscurely. Thus Euripides says, "The mind (νοῦς) of the dead is not alive, yet hath it immortal consciousness, when it hath been merged in the immortal ether."[1] And again, "Let each depart into the element from which it came, the spirit to the ether, the body to the earth."[2] Similarly Virgil[3] speaks of the Deity who pervades the earth and the wide ocean and the vault of heaven, the Deity from whom the flocks and herds and men and all wild beasts do draw at birth the subtle, vital air, and into whom at length they all return and are resolved.

But it is in the writings of the Stoics that the doctrine of the Universal Soul becomes most frequent and authoritative. Thus Epictetus says of death: "God gives the signal for retreat, opens the

[1] *Helena*, 1014. [2] *Supplices*, 532. [3] *Georgics*, iv. 221–226.

door and says to you, Go. Go whither? To nothing terrible, but to the place from which you came, to your friends and kinsmen, to the elements: what there was in you of fire goes to fire; of earth to earth; of air (spirit) to air (ὅσον πνευματίου εἰς πνευμάτιον); of water to water; no Hades nor Acheron nor Cocytus nor Pyriphlegethon, but all is full of Gods and Daemons."[1] So, too, Marcus Aurelius: "If souls continue to exist, how does the air contain them from Eternity? But how does the earth contain the bodies of those who have been buried from time so remote? For, as here, the mutation of these bodies after a certain continuance, whatever it may be, and their dissolution make room for other dead bodies, so the souls which are removed into the air after subsisting for some time are transmuted and diffused and assume a fiery nature by being received into the seminal intelligence of the Universe, and in this way make room for the fresh souls which come to dwell there."[2]

The Stoics were indeed divided in opinion, some holding that the individual soul would at death be

---

[1] *The Discourses of Epictetus*, translated by Long. Book iii., chap. 13.
[2] *The Thoughts of the Emperor M. Aurelius Antoninus*, translated by Long. Book iv. § 21.

immediately reabsorbed into the Universal Soul, others that it would retain its individuality until the final conflagration, which was an article of the Stoic creed, and would then be reabsorbed; but that the individual soul, as it had emanated from the Universal Soul, so into it would be soon or late reabsorbed, was a general doctrine of the Stoic philosophy.

It is curious that this doctrine of the soul's survival after death, *i.e.*, of its temporary survival as distinct from its Immortality, has been asserted in modern times by some few thinkers, though they have expressed themselves rather hesitatingly, and the ultimate destiny of the soul as they conceived it, where it has fallen short of Immortality, has been not reabsorption but annihilation. They are chiefly the religious thinkers who, while postulating Immortality for the souls of the virtuous, have seemed to find by a strange rational process, in the idea that other souls would enjoy a qualified or limited Immortality (if it may be so spoken of), a halfway house between Immortality which they conceived as being the recompense of virtue, and annihilation as the penal destiny of vice. But they have been few, and it has been felt that they had been driven into a logical difficulty by their denial of the absolute Immortality of all souls.

The doctrine of reabsorption, or in other words the belief that the individual soul is in the moment of death reabsorbed into the Universal Soul stands on firmer philosophical ground, and it has been held even by some Christian authorities. In one of Schleiermacher's letters (which has lately been quoted by Dr. Martineau[1]) an attempt is made to present the doctrine as if it were equivalent to the truth revealed by Christ. To a lady whose heart was torn by longing for personal reunion in the future life with the young husband taken from her soon after their marriage, he wrote : " When your imagination brings before you the idea of a melting away into the great All, let it not, dear child, lay on you any touch of bitter sorrow. Do but think of it as a merging not into death, but into life, and that the highest life. It is indeed that after which we all strive in this life, only that we never reach it, viz., to live simply in the Divine Whole to which we belong, and to put away from us the pretension to set up for ourselves, as if we could be our own. If he now is living in God, and you love him eter-

---

[1] *A Study of Religion*, vol. ii. pp. 335, *sqq.*

nally in God, as you loved and knew God in him, can you think of anything sublimer and more glorious? Is not this the highest end of love, in comparison with which everything which clings only to the personal life and arises thence is nothing?"

Such is the doctrine of reabsorption, as put forward by one whose life was illuminated by many beautiful graces of the Christian character; and if any one could recommend it by personal authority, it would be he. Philosophically, indeed, it is incontestable. But it is not the doctrine so dear to human hearts. It breaks down just where it is most needed as a satisfaction for the sorrows and shortcomings of Humanity. All the comfort which the doctrine of Immortality affords is dependent upon the continuance of individuality. To lose individuality—to be merged soon or late, in the Infinite Whole is, according to the conscience of men, to forfeit the boon of the Immortal Life. It is Pantheism, not Christianity. It touches the mind, but it cannot touch the heart. By the graveside, where the mourners lay their loved ones to rest, it is felt to be impotent and vain. It is such doctrine as may issue from the life of a Spinoza, but it fails in the presence of Christ. It is not the doctrine for which this Essay is a plea.

III. Again, the Immortality for which I plead is not conditional but absolute. I do not urge that Immortality is attainable, but that it is actual; not that it is partial, but that it is universal; not that it may be, but that it is. It has been already intimated that some modern thinkers, under the pressure of logical difficulties which they had commonly made for themselves, have been led to argue, though as a rule faintheartedly, for a conditional Immortality, *i.e.*, for the Immortality of some souls under certain conditions and not of all souls intrinsically. But this too is an old-world theory, like so many others. No idea is more usual among savage peoples, where Immortality is believed in at all, than that it is certain privileged souls alone which will be Immortal. But while Immortality, if regarded as conditional, has in the modern world been assumed to be the privilege of virtue, it was assumed by savage peoples to be the privilege of rank. For to savages who are naturally disposed to look upon the future life not as a compensation or retribution for the present, but as a mere continuation of the present life (the idea of future retribution being much later) it seems a thing of course that the aristocracy of the world which they know should be prolonged into the world which they do not know; and as existence after death is itself in their eyes a privilege and not (as in this world) a common possession, they conclude that the warriors and chiefs will live again, but the common people will lie in their graves eternally.

It is true that this belief is not consistently maintained; sometimes the kinsfolk or servants of a chief, or even his animals, are said to possess a life immortal as his own. But the reason of their Immortality will be found to lie not in their nature but in their relation to the master whom they serve; and it is in order to do him service that they are gifted with Immortality, as when the faithful dog of the Red Indian warrior was slain by his grave in the belief that, when he came to the happy hunting grounds of the Blessed, he would find his dog at his side. Such practices as Suttee in India are witnesses to the belief in this Immortality (if I may call it so) of relation. They do not signify the Immortality of all men — still less of all living creatures; but they enhance the power and dignity of the Immortality inherent in the great men. That Immortality, as has been said, belongs to greatness, not to goodness.

But modern thought, in so far as it has made Immortality conditional, has found its condition in virtue. It is the good who live for ever; the wicked perish. That is the doctrine of some theologians; it is the tacit assumption of a good many Christians. It may be supported (like almost any other belief) by isolated passages of Holy Scripture, though the interpreters of these passages have sometimes confused the final destruction of evil, which is an admittedly Christian doctrine, with the destruction of individual sinners; but it runs counter to the teaching of Scripture as a whole. We shall see hereafter what has been the attitude of the Church and of the most eminent of the Fathers towards the doctrine of conditional Immortality. It is enough to say now that it could not be believed by any Christian except upon the authority of direct Revelation. For the idea of a conditional Immortality—*i.e.*, of an Immortality which may or may not be, and which is the attribute of some but not of all—cuts away the main supports of the belief in Immortality itself. For apart from Revelation (which is out of court in a general religious argument) the belief in the Immortality of the soul principally depends upon the soul's intrinsic nature. It is because Immortality is the natural property of the human soul that the thought of its destruction is intolerable and impossible. Neither philosophy nor religion possesses the means (apart from Revelation) of making a distinction between souls in respect of their Immortality. The argument which proves the soul immortal, proves all souls immortal. "The unconditional destiny of all men," says Bishop Martensen, "is Immortality."[1] But what becomes of this destiny, if Immortality is conditioned by human merit or demerit, if it is the lot of some souls and not of others, if it is not an absolute intrinsic quality of human nature? No doubt a direct revelation, if it were explicit and authoritative, might prove what is called conditional Immortality, but it would destroy nearly all the evidences for Immortality except that of the revelation itself. It is the object of this essay to show, as far as possible, that the soul which is in every man is immortal.

[1] *Christian Dogmatics*, § 274.

IV. But if the various theories of Immortality which have been considered are thus put aside, it can hardly be necessary to say that there is no room within the scope of this Essay for that strange illogical view of the Immortal Life which is taught in the Positivist Creed. "Words," says Bacon, "as a Tartar's bow, do shoot back upon the understanding of the wisest, and mightily entangle and pervert the judgment, so as it is almost necessary in all controversies and disputations to imitate the wisdom of the mathematicians in setting down in the very beginning the definitions of our words and terms, that others may know how we accept and understand them, and whether they concur with us or no." But I know no more striking example of the influence which words, even when the life is gone out of them, still exercise upon the human mind than that the word "Immortality," like the word "religion" itself, should be cherished and usurped by thinkers, who have robbed it of all its native force and dignity.

Comte himself indeed, in speaking of the Positivist Immortality, or (as he preferred to call it) "the subjective life," generally employed language that veiled its paradox in a certain sentimental ambiguity. Thus, in reference to the cry of Danton on the scaffold, " Perish my memory, only let my country be free !" he says : "Even in this heroic cry we trace the idea that the outward reward of a great life extends to its subjective Immortality. He who has truly lived for others should hope to live on, in and by others. This subjective return is purer at once and surer than the objective, for it carries on the services rendered and perfects the judgment of those services. Under the impulse given by the Positivist spirit, spontaneously and systematically, this noble recompense is accessible to all who are capable of understanding it and deserving it."[1]

Comte's disciples have, as often happens, gone beyond their master ; they have filled in his shadowy outlines of religion, they have clothed his skeleton of Immortality in the phrases of a beautiful and touching poetry. It is to this investiture that it owes what grace or charm it has. Many persons who would scorn such an Immortality as Comte offers find an echo in their

[1] *System of Positive Polity*, vol. iv. chap. i., p. 45, Congreve's Translation.

hearts (and it is a nobly unselfish echo) to George Eliot's eloquent lines—

> " O may I join the choir invisible,
> Of those immortal dead who live again
> In minds made better by their presence, . . .
> . . . . So to live is heaven.
> To make undying music in the world,
> Breathing as beauteous order that controls
> With growing sway the growing life of man.
> . . . . . This is life to come,
> Which martyred men have made more glorious
> For us who strive to follow."

and what they appreciate they fancy they believe. But this is not a doctrine which can bear the scrutiny of close thought. It is playing with names, playing with facts. It is taking, or trying to take, the shadow for the substance. An Immortality of being remembered is no Immortality except in metaphor. Regret is not life; and even if it were, what would then be the Immortality of those souls (than whom none are more sacred upon earth) whose virtue is never heard of nor ever dreamt of—the souls that live and die in obscurity and do good by stealth and suffer many things for others, though they thank them not and often revile them, and are only seen by Him who "seeth in secret"? The Positivist Creed fails; for it makes

Immortality to depend upon the judgment of men, and for the most part we judge each other wrongly, if at all. It is not for a hope like this that the heart of Man is athirst; and I put it aside in this essay.

The Immortality for which I plead is the personal, intrinsic, inalienable, eternal attribute of every individual soul of man. But what is the soul?

This is evidently an important question; it is the most important question with which this Essay deals. For the doctrine that the soul survives after death, and survives eternally, possesses little value, unless it be known what is the nature of the soul. But if the nature of the soul as it is in itself, without regard to limiting material conditions, is ascertained, it will be possible to form some estimate of the life that is proper to the soul when emancipated from the body.

Human nature is divisible into parts. It is not necessary to consider whether the division is ultimately reasonable or not. We are not considering human nature as it is in the sight of God; we are considering it as men speak and think of it.

The common speech of mankind treats body and soul together as the equivalent of Man's whole being. If it is said that a person is ruined "body and soul," the meaning is that the ruin is complete.

About the word "body" there is no doubt or difficulty. It has always and everywhere signified the same thing. But the English word "soul," or the word which corresponds to it in some other languages, has not always been used in the same sense. We do not, it would seem, use it uniformly even now. Thus it may be doubted whether we mean the same thing, *i.e.*, the same part of man's composite being, when we say that a person's soul is given to music or art, as when we say that his soul is in God's keeping.

The only way of arriving at a definition of the word "soul" is, I think, to examine it historically.

The philosophers of ancient Greece were the first persons who occupied themselves with the scientific and logical treatment of the soul. The Greek word usually translated "soul"—the word ψυχή—was not yet solidified when it came into the hands of Plato and Aristotle; it was in a sort of fluid state, and they could more or less mould it at will. Still it possessed a certain definite signification.

Greek thought recognised in human nature body and soul. It understood by the body the material substance which is visible and tangible, and which is laid after death in the grave. It understood by the soul all that is not body. But for a long time it did not inquire how the non-corporeal part of human nature should be defined.

It is clear, however, that, if the ψυχή or "soul" were an equivalent expression for all that is not corporeal in human nature, it would possess a very wide range of meaning. It might be predicated of beings, and even of inanimate things, which would not be looked upon in the modern world as having souls. Thus Aristotle quotes a saying of Thales, the first of the celebrated Seven Wise Men of Greece, that "the magnet must have a soul (ψυχή), for it attracts iron." He himself speaks of the "soul" (ψυχή) of a plant, understanding no more by it than the vital principle, which is the source of growth and fertility. Similarly he speaks of the "soul" of an animal as, *e.g.*, of a horse or a dog; and here the ψυχή is higher and nobler than in a plant, as it includes not life alone but instinct, appetite and affection; but it is not yet all that is understood by "soul" to-day. It would be difficult to put the Aristotelian view more exactly than in Grote's words, "The varieties of soul are distributed into successive stages, gradually narrowing in extension and enlarging in comprehension; the first or lowest stage being co-extensive with the whole, but connoting only two or three simple attributes; the second or next above connoting all these and more besides, but denoting only part of the individuals denoted by the first; the third connoting all this and more, but denoting yet fewer individuals, and so forward. Thus the concrete individuals, called living bodies, include all plants as well as all animals; but the soul, called Nutritive by Aristotle, corresponding thereto connotes only nutrition, growth, decay, and generation of another similar individual. In the second stage, plants are left out, but all animals remain; the Sentient soul, belonging to animals, but not belonging to any plants connotes all the functions and faculties of the Nutritive soul, together with sensible perception (at least in its rudest shape) besides. We proceed onward in the same direction, taking in additional faculties —the Movent, Appetitive, Phantastic (Imaginative) Noetic (Intelligent) soul, and thus diminishing the total of individuals denoted. But each higher variety of soul continues to possess all the faculties of the lower. Thus the Sentient soul cannot exist without comprehending all the faculties of the Nutritive, though the Nutritive exists (in plants) without any admixture of the Sentient. Again, the Sentient soul does not necessarily possess either memory, imagination, or intellect (*Noûs*), but no soul can be either Imaginative or Noetic without being Sentient as well as Nutritive. The Noetic soul, as the highest of all, retains in itself all the lower faculties, but these are found to exist apart from it."[1]

There is then a ψυχή or "soul" of men as well as of the lower animals or of plants, and it is in a fuller sense a soul; for it is the seat not of the vital principle only nor of the appetite and affection only, but of the rational and moral faculties. Aristotle calls it the intelligent or ratiocinative soul. It is the part of human nature which in the Aristotelian philosophy is supreme.

As a Greek, although the wisest of the Greeks, Aristotle recognised, and could recognise, nothing higher than this intellectual soul. His philoso-

[1] Grote, Aristotle, vol. ii., chap. xii. p. 191.

phical doctrine of the soul is the highest of which Greek thought was capable.

It can now be seen that the ψυχή or "soul" as conceived by the Greeks possessed three several meanings which may be ranged, as it were, in an ascending scale of dignity. If it were necessary to find English equivalents for them (though the equivalence cannot be exact) they might perhaps be taken as "life," "sense," and "reason." For "life" may naturally represent the vital principle, "sense" the emotional, and "reason" the intellectual or ratiocinative. But in the Greek, and specially the Aristotelian uses of "soul," the higher meaning, as it was developed, included the lower; it was not something generically different from the lower, but was always that and something added to it, and although the something so added was infinitely the greater part of the soul in its new meaning, it was not the whole.

Thus the ψυχή of a plant was its life, or, more strictly, its principle of growth and fertility.

The ψυχή of an animal was its life *plus* its sentient or appetitive principle; it was primarily the sense and only in a secondary degree the life, but strictly considered it was made up of both.

The ψυχή of a man was his life or vital principle and his sentient or appetitive principle, but it was above all his intellectual principle or reason.

Beyond this point, as has been said, the Greek thought, and therefore the Greek conception of the soul, did not go. The reason was the "end" or supreme part of human nature.

If we pass now to the Hebrew Scriptures, as interpreted by the harmonious voices of the Jewish and Christian religions, we are struck by a difference in the conception or estimate of human nature. It corresponds to the difference between the Greek and the Hebrew characters. To the Greek, reason was the highest thing; its supremacy could not be disputed. But it was not the highest thing to the Hebrew. He had not apprehended the supreme truths of life, nor did he expect any one to apprehend them, by a process of the reason. "Canst thou by wisdom find out God?" is a question issuing from the very heart of Jewish religious thought. No Jew could have hesitated as to the answer which it required. The desire of the Jewish nation was for God. The Hebrew psalmists and prophets give repeated expression to that desire.

"As the hart panteth after the waterbrooks," *i.e.*, as the hart pursued by huntsmen on the mountains longs for a refreshing draught, "so panteth my soul after Thee, O God."[1] "O God, Thou art my God; early will I seek Thee: my soul thirsteth for Thee, my flesh longeth for Thee, in a dry and thirsty land where no water is."[2] But it was not reason which inspired, or could satisfy, the passion of the Hebrew soul for God. In the Hebrew view, reason, if it stood by itself, neither prevented nor ensured the knowledge of God. It was in another way, by another faculty than the reason, that God and Divine things came to be known. What that faculty was the Scriptures of the Old Testament intimate, though but faintly; in the New Testament it is defined and explained.

We shall find the explanation in St. Paul's writings.

The theology of St. Paul may be said to represent the Hebrew conception of human nature in its highest form. St. Paul was by birth and education a Jew, but he had studied in the Greek University of Tarsus, and he was familiar with the language and literature of Greece. The limitations of his

[1] Psalm xlii. 1. [2] Psalm lxiii. 1.

intellectual scope had been enlarged by philosophy, but his imagination was controlled by religious awe. In him therefore, far better than in Philo, Hebrew and Greek thought found a meeting-place. Considering that St. Paul had never spoken to and indeed had never seen in the flesh the Master to whose service he consecrated his life, I think his intellectual influence upon Christian theology (though sometimes exaggerated, as by Renan) ought to be regarded as one of the marvels of speculative history. But his intellectual powers were sublime; he scanned with penetrating vision the depths of Divine truth; the eighteen centuries of Christianity have not exhausted the profundity of his teaching; and apart altogether from the spiritual intuitions and revelations which he claimed as his personal experiences, it is doubtful if the Christian or pagan world has ever produced a thinker of more acute and subtle intellect than his.

St. Paul's view of human nature is different from Aristotle's. In his view human nature consists of three parts or elements, which are distinct.

The first of these is the σῶμα or "body," and it is what has been always understood by the body.

The second is the ψυχή or "soul," including the

life, the sense, the affection or appetite and the reason.

The third is the πνεῦμα or "spirit," *i.e.*, the faculty by which Man apprehends God.

It appears, then, that St. Paul adds the "spirit" or spiritual part of human nature to the parts enumerated by Aristotle. That is the faculty which, as the Hebrew Scriptures implicitly taught, places Man in relation to his Maker. And as constituting or creating this Divine relation, that faculty is in human nature supreme.

It is important to observe what a light this tripartition of human nature seems to shed upon the facts of human life and human thought.

The three parts are logically distinct; each exists and may be developed independently of the others. To assume that the cultivation of one part necessarily improves or corroborates the others, or either of the others, is to misunderstand the Pauline theology.

Suppose, *e.g.*, that the body of a man is developed by exercise and discipline; the development is a good thing in itself, but it does not necessarily or naturally imply a corresponding development of the soul (ψυχή). Thus a man may be a brilliant athlete but a poor thinker. It is not said that athletic energy and logical acumen are not found together, they may or may not coexist; it is enough that the one does not imply the other.

Or, again, suppose that the soul and especially that part of it which is highest, viz., the reason, is fully developed; the development is good in itself, but it does not imply a corresponding development of the πνεῦμα or "spirit." Just as the athlete is not necessarily a thinker, so the thinker is not necessarily a saint.

It may indeed be suggested, not without some apparent reason, that the equal and simultaneous culture of all the parts of human nature is itself a difficulty, and that, where one is highly cultivated, the others are apt to be proportionately enfeebled. But this suggestion St. Paul does not make. His argument turns simply upon the way in which Humanity becomes cognisant of Divine truth. He is not concerned with historical revelations, which are evidently liable, in some at least of their aspects, to the judgment of the intellect, but with the personal consciousness of God. He realises the fact, not less conspicuous in modern than in ancient times, that, where two persons possess equal ability, equal information and equal character, to one the Being of God may be a doubt or a paradox or an absurdity, and to the other it may be the most luminous of truths. The line of demarcation between these persons and between others like them, whatever it is, is not intellectual; but the one is religious because he possesses, and the other is non-religious because he does not possess, something that is not intellect, and yet *ex hypothesi* can sit in judgment upon a problem of the soul.

That something is the faculty which St. Paul calls πνεῦμα or "spirit."

The relation of the Spirit of God to the spirit or spiritual faculty in Man, is a cardinal matter in the Pauline theology. It can only be alluded to here.

Between the Spirit of God and the spirit of man there is in St. Paul's view a correspondence or intercommunion. The Divine Spirit "beareth witness with our spirit, that we are the children of God." The Divine Spirit "helpeth our infirmities." He "maketh intercession for us."[1] He is the earnest as He is the attestation of the future blessings reserved for those who are called the "saints" or the "sons of God."

[1] Romans viii. 16, 26.

But the activity of the Divine Spirit in the souls of men is contingent upon the sympathetic activity of the spiritual faculty in men themselves. The spiritual faculty may be cultivated, illumined, purified by human co-operation with the Divine Spirit until men enjoy the perfect vision of God. Or, again, it may be starved and atrophied by neglect; then men become at last incapable of seeing Him.

For "the natural" (or psychical) "man" in St. Paul's words, *i.e.*, the ψυχικὸς ἄνθρωπος, the man of ψυχή or "soul," but not of πνεῦμα or "spirit," "receiveth not the things of the Spirit of God, ... neither can he know them, because they are spiritually discerned."[1] To one whose spiritual faculty is dead the Being of God is as sunlight to the blind, or as music to the deaf. But to the spiritual man it is the truth of truths, the joy of joys.

This is St. Paul's philosophical account of human nature. Thus, in his view, the trinity of human nature is complete. Man—the three in one—is made in the image of the Triune God. "I pray God," he says, writing to the Thessalonians of human nature regarded as a whole, "your whole

[1] 1 Corinthians ii. 14.

spirit and soul and body be preserved blameless unto the coming of our Lord Jesus Christ."[1]

It would seem proper, then, to speak of human nature as threefold, and no doubt that is the strictly philosophical, as it is also the strictly religious, manner of speech; but the tripartition is not always observed. For ψυχή or "soul" may denote all that is not spiritual in human nature; it may be set as a single comprehensive term against πνεῦμα or "spirit," and then, but only then, it includes the body. Or ψυχή may be, and often is, used, in contrast with σῶμα, to denote all the parts of human nature that are not in themselves visible and material; and in this use it includes not the life only, nor the life and the appetite only, nor the life the appetite and the reason only, but the spirit. It is so when "body and soul" are treated as representative of the whole human being. It is so, when the soul is taken, as in our Lord's teaching, to signify the part which is most sacred and sublime in human nature; for that is clearly not the appetite or the reason, but the spirit, the eternal element, the part which is immediately related to God.

We see, then, that the word ψυχή, or "soul,"

[1] 1 Thessalonians v. 23.

possesses two meanings, a narrower meaning in which it stands for the life, the appetite and the reason, and a larger meaning in which it includes the spirit as well. Nay, the spirit is so transcendently important in view of Immortality that, when it is included, it tends to overshadow the other attributes or faculties of human nature, it usurps or tends to usurp to itself the whole meaning of "soul." This is the case in the Greek language, but it is the case in English also. When we speak of a man's "soul," or of his "spirit," we generally mean the same thing, *i.e.*, the part of him which is invisible and immortal. We may say indiscriminately that in death his "soul" has departed, or his "spirit." So true is this that while the body has an adjective "bodily" corresponding to it, and the spirit has "spiritual," there is in English no adjective corresponding to "soul"; for "psychical" is a late invention and its meaning is not in fact co-extensive with the "soul." The adjective "spiritual" does duty for the soul as well as the spirit in many uses, because the "spirit" and the "soul" of a man as commonly understood are one and the same. It is convenient, however, as well as correct, to make a distinction between them. In this Essay, when I speak of "spirit," I shall mean the spiritual faculty alone; when I speak of "soul," I shall mean the whole invisible, immaterial part of human nature, *i.e.*, the life, the sense, the reason and the spirit. For the union of life, sense and reason, apart from the spirit, there is no English word. Perhaps the word least inappropriate would be " nature."

The distinction between the soul, or more properly the being, and the spirit is not essential, as will, I think, appear, in the treatment of human Immortality. Still, it cannot be ignored without some loss.

It is now possible to ask, What is the element or part of human nature which is believed to survive the grave and to last for ever? The answer to that question will throw a light upon the nature of Immortality itself. For the scope or destiny of the Immortal Life must apparently be determined by the nature of the subject which is endowed with Immortality. The ancient story of Tithonus who was said to have obtained the gift of eternal life, but not of eternal youth, is a witness that Immortality is not a boon, unless certain graces or faculties are implied in it. In other words, Immortality is conditioned by the nature of the immortal being.

What is it, then, which survives or is immortal?

In order to see what is the immortal part of human nature, it will be well to refer once more, however briefly, to the contrast between the pagan and Christian conceptions of Immortality. In the pagan world the thought of Immortality or of the soul's survival after death, even when it was accepted as possible or probable, inspired no happiness. There was no anticipation or exultation in the prospect of a future life. The best and wisest of the ancient Greeks, with the possible exception of a few philosophers, such as Socrates, if it had been open to them to choose or refuse the gift of Immortality, would have refused it. That Immortality could be the satisfaction of human desires, or the compensation for human sufferings, or the reward of human virtues, was an idea that did not occur to them, and would not have been intelligible to their minds. Immortality did not appear to them as a joyful hope, but as a bad dream, or a painful necessity, or at the best a tolerable fate.

Let me illustrate this feeling of the pagan world by quoting two passages taken, as it were, the one from the dawn, the other from the sunset of classical literature.

It is well known how in the *Odyssey* of Homer

Odysseus goes down to the lower world and, meeting Achilles there, seeks to comfort him in his death, by telling him that, as he had been honoured like a god while he lived upon the earth, so, too, he was a mighty prince among the dead. But Achilles makes answer—

"Speak not comfortably to me of death, O great Odysseus. Rather would I live on ground as the hireling of another, with a landless man who has no great livelihood, than bear sway among all the dead that be departed." [1]

What a witness is such language as this to the gloom of the destiny (as Homer conceived it) reserved in the after-life for the most exalted and distinguished of mankind!

The other passage shall be the familiar address of the Emperor Hadrian to his own departing soul, an address which has often been translated; but it may here be given in the original Latin, and in the English of Matthew Prior.

"Animula vagula blandula
Hospes comesque corporis,
Quae nunc abibis in loca
Pallidula, rigida, nudula,
Nec, ut soles, dabis jocos?"

[1] *Odyssey*, xi. 489. The translation is that of Messrs. Butcher and Lang.

> "Poor little pretty fluttering thing,
>   Must we no longer live together?
> And dost thou prune thy trembling wing;
>   To take thy flight, thou know'st not whither?
> Thy humorous vein, thy pleasing folly,
>   Lies all neglected, all forgot;
> And pensive, wavering, melancholy,
>   Thou dread'st and hop'st thou know'st not what."

Can any words be more sorrowful or more hopeless? There is in them no sense of gain, but all is loss. The very diminutives imply the vanity of the soul's existence. Not a word suggests that the soul, as soon as it is emancipated from the body, will enter upon a larger life. It is earth which is heaven to the Emperor; the future is darkness. How strange too, how significant is the phrase,

> "Nec, ut soles, dabis jocos,"

as if the highest quality of the soul were "pleasing folly"!

Is it possible to explain the gloom which hangs as a pall over the anticipation of a future life from the beginning to the end of pagan history?

The explanation lies in the conception of the soul. In Homer's poetry the soul which is deemed to survive the body is little more than the mere vital principle. The life of Achilles, "the divine son of

Peleus," in Hades is a life of mere existence, a life without powers or passions, a life that is only a shadow of the earthly life. But a life devoid of hope, solace, affection or imagination can scarce be regarded as a boon. It is a life of the ψυχή in its lowest, or all but its lowest, sense.

Nor is it to a much higher level of religious philosophy that the Emperor Hadrian's thought ascends so late as in the second century of the Christian era. He, too, looks for existence, but for little more. His soul, when it leaves the body whose guest and companion it has been, will lack the warmth, the grace, the joyousness which have clothed it in life. The Emperor Hadrian was not an ordinary man; he had played a great part in history, his mind had been elevated by dignity and solemnised by responsibility, and this was his whole idea of the life after death. What could the future seem to him but dark and sad? His voice is the highest perhaps of political paganism. He believed (if indeed he did believe) in a life reaching beyond the grave, but it was a life bereft of all that makes this life worth living, and in spite of himself he shrank from it with pain.

Homer and Hadrian may be taken as representing

the general sentiment of the pagan world at different stages in regard to the prospect of the soul's Immortality. But they do not represent the highest speculation. The religious teachers of classical antiquity were not the priests; they were first the poets, and afterwards the philosophers. Let us then appeal to the greatest and best of the philosophers, to Socrates.

The teaching of Socrates upon the future of the soul is represented, at its highest elevation, by the Platonic dialogue which bears the name of his beloved disciple, the *Phædo*. The *Phædo* stands among the masterpieces of human literature. It is one of those works in which the perfect harmony of the subject and of the circumstances in which it is treated, create an indelible impression. "Nobody," says Socrates, with his quiet irony, "can pretend that I am talking of what does not concern me at this time." And the dignity of Socrates himself, his impressive serenity, his love of philosophical discussion, strong even in death, his abiding personal faith in the future of wise and holy souls, have united to win for the Dialogue of the Immortal Life, as the *Phædo* may be justly called, an Immortality as true as the subject with which it deals.

But it is not with the Socratic arguments for

Immortality that I am concerned; they will claim consideration in a later chapter. It is with the nature of Immortality as Socrates conceived it.

The soul which Socrates in the *Phædo* called immortal is not the soul or spirit of the Christian doctrine. It is more than the vital principle, but less than the spiritual principle, in man; it is the mind, the seat of the desire, affection, and reason, but chiefly of the reason; for in the eyes of Socrates the reason was the highest of human faculties; to know right was necessarily to do it; dialectic was the end of life, and dialectical communion with the elect souls in the world beyond the grave was the supreme intellectual satisfaction. He who thought that virtue was knowledge could look for no higher end than the perfecting of knowledge by discussion. Rational existence, existence chastened and elevated by reason, was the goal, as of his belief, so also of his desire. Thus it was that his anticipation of the future life was not, like the pagan poet's, sombre and regretful, nor like the Christian saint's, rapturous and ecstatic; it was simply and calmly acquiescent in a destiny which, if it were not a dream, would surely in the nature of things be better, as being more rational, more intellectual than the present. But it might be a dream, and the fear that it might be is apparent in the *Phædo*, underlying the very arguments that seek to dispel it; and in the *Apology* the last words of Socrates are these: "The hour of departure has arrived, and we go our ways, I to die, and you to live. Which is better God only knows."

How different from this is the language of Christian belief! It will be enough to cite such passages as St. Paul's: "To me to live is Christ, to die is gain," "For I am in a strait betwixt two, having a desire to depart and to be with Christ, which is far better";[1] or, "I have fought a good fight, I have finished my course, I have kept the faith; henceforth there is laid up for me a crown of righteousness which the Lord, the righteous Judge, shall give me at that day, and not to me only, but unto them also that love His appearing";[2] or, St. John's: "It doth not yet appear what we shall be: but we know that when He shall appear we shall be like Him; for we shall see Him as He is."[3] And the difference is that, when the soul is conceived, as it is by the Christian Apostles, to be not only sentient and intellectual,

[1] Philippians i. 21–23.   [2] 2 Timothy iv. 18.
[3] 1 John iii. 2.

but above all to be spiritual, then alone is it felt to be capable of the joy, the rapture, the beatitude of communion with the Father of Spirits.

To this beatitude we shall return in the last chapter. For the present we are concerned with the nature of Immortality. And in view of Immortality (apart of course from Revelation) it would seem that the distinction between body and soul, *i.e.*, between the material and the immaterial parts of human nature is fundamental; but it is not so with the distinction between what is psychical or of the soul, and what is spiritual in human nature. The confusion of " soul " and " spirit," or more properly the comprehension of "spirit" under "soul," is a witness to the interlacing of the two concepts. " Soul " includes " spirit," as has been said ; it is sometimes used for " spirit." Whether the spirit is a principle distinct from the affection and reason, or the same principle is on the one side appetitive and logical, and on the other side spiritual, is not essential to the doctrine of Immortality.

St. Paul's tripartition of human nature may affect the character, but not the fact, of the Immortal Life. Apart from the soul, the body is incapable of thought and worship. But there is in human nature something which is not the body—an entity opposed to the body and superior to the body—something which is the very life or being of the individual; in a word, which is himself. Dr. Martineau defines it clearly when he says: "This constant centre to which we refer all our acts as their source, and all our experiences as their receptacle, is what we mean by the soul."[1]

It remains to ask, then, What is presumably the change effected by death?

Death is dissolution, but it is the dissolution not of mind and spirit, so far as present experience tells, but of body and soul; for it is the body alone which is left behind at death, the body which dies, and all else that constitutes being passes into eternity.

As is the fate of the affection or the desire in death, so is that of the reason, and so, too, that of the spirit. Death works the same effect upon all. What survives or passes at death out of human cognition is the whole immaterial part of human nature, or in one word, the soul.

And herein lies the answer (so far as any can be given) to the question, In what does identity consist? Not in the body of a man, it is clear; for the material

[1] *A Study of Religion*, vol. ii. p. 330.

particles constituting the body are for ever undergoing change. It is the persistency of the life, the reason, the spirit, that makes the man, and of these the seat is the soul; and the soul, if it survive the grave (as argument shows), not only constitutes identity in this life, but continues and conserves it in the life to come.

The seat of human identity is the soul. It is the man himself who lives after death if the soul is immortal. His mental, moral, and spiritual powers survive. It is only the vesture of his powers—the body—the least and lowest part of him—that dies. In his soul is the principle of life.

There are certain inferences flowing from the true conception of the soul's nature; and they may properly be indicated here.

1. The soul is immortal, *i.e.*, everlasting.

It does not merely survive death, or a series of deaths; it survives everlastingly. It survives in virtue of the character which distinguishes it from all that is dissoluble and destructible. It possesses in itself the potency of an unending existence. It partakes of the Immortal Nature, which is centred and consummated in God, and, as partaking of that Nature, it is gifted with Immortality.

2. The soul, as it is immortal, is immaterial.

This may seem to be a truth which it is needless to emphasise. We do not naturally think of the soul as in any sense substantial. We can realise, or we imagine that we can realise, pure spirit. Yet there has been no greater difficulty in human thought than the intellectual emancipation of spirit from matter. "The ancients," says Dr. Döllinger, "understood by the soul a kind of secretion or evaporation of brain, blood, or heart, or a sort of respiration. They described it as a subtle aerial or fiery substance, or conceived it to be a mere quality, like the harmony of a musical instrument, which was lost in the dissolution of the body."[1] In Homer, for example, the soul is imagined as a vapour or smoke or similar to these. Thus Achilles puts forth his hands to seize the spirit or soul of Patroclus, but in vain; for "the soul had sped *like a vapour* gibbering beneath the earth."[2] Similarly in Virgil Eurydice fades from the sight of Orpheus, "mingling *as the smoke* with the thin air."[3] Modern fancy even now clothes the spirit or ghost with the form of humanity. Modern supersti-

---

[1] *The Gentile and the Jew*, vol. ii. p. 144, Darnell's Translation.
[2] *Iliad*, xxiii. 100.   [3] *Georgics*, iv. 499.

tion requires the doors or windows of the death-chamber to be opened at death, that the spirit may depart in peace.

Not such is the Christian doctrine of Immortality, although the fathers of the Church have sometimes failed to comprehend it in its integrity, as when Tertullian argued that, if the soul were not material, it could not act upon the body nor be acted upon by it.[1] It is with a finer perception that Dante makes the spirits in his Purgatorio tremble at finding that his body, unlike their own, casts a shadow on the ground.

> "Feriami il Sole in su l'omero destro
> Che già, raggiando, tutto l'occidente
> Mutava in bianco aspetto di cilestro ;
> Ed io facea con l'ombra più rovente
> Parer la fiamma ; e pure a tanto indizio
> Vidi molt' ombre, andando, poner mente.
> Questa fu la cagion che diede inizio
> Loro a parlar di me, e cominciarsi
> A dir :—' Colui non par corpo fittizio." '

> "The sun
> Now all the western clime irradiate chang'd
> From azure tinct to white ; and as I pass'd,
> My passing shadow made the umber'd flame
> Burn ruddier. At so strange a sight I mark'd

---

[1] *De Anima*, chap. v.

> That many a spirit marvel'd on his way.
> This bred occasion first to speak of me,
> 'He seems,' said they, 'no insubstantial frame.' " [1]

3. Another point which emerges clearly upon consideration is that the Immortality of the lower animals (if it exists) must be something essentially different from human Immortality. What are the arguments for Immortality, and how far, if they hold good for men, they will hold good also for the lower animals is a question which will be considered in its place. All that need be said here is that the nature of Immortality must depend upon the nature of the soul. Now the lower animals consist of a material element, viz., the body which remains at death, like the human body, and decays, and also of certain immaterial elements or principles, viz., the life, the sense, the appetite and (under certain limitations) the reason, but not of spirit. The Immortality then of the lower animals, if they are endowed with it at all, may well be such as allows of life, movement, desire and instinctive action; but it cannot be more than this, unless in virtue of some special Divine operation, such as the original creation of life upon the earth, or the birth

---

[1] *Purgatorio*, Canto xxvi., Cary's Translation. The same thought occurs in Cantos v. and xxv.

of the individual soul within the embryo; it cannot be in itself a life of the spirit, and therefore it cannot admit of the spiritual prerogatives of worship or rapture or communion with God.

4. There is another inference not less important, which results from the true conception of human nature as a whole. We are too apt to suppose that the only part of human nature which survives the grave is the spirit, though we speak of it as the " soul." We have pictured to ourselves the Immortal Life as circumscribed by the duties and prerogatives of devotion; we have not thought of it as affording any scope for the play of intellect or passion. But the soul has been shown to be intellectual and moral as well as spiritual; it must therefore be capable of intellectual and moral activities. It is not only the disposition to virtue, it is equally the disposition to learning and affection, which transcends death. Whatever seed of knowledge or dutifulness or industry or virtue is sown in this life will bear fruit in Immortality.

This is the solemnising, inspiring lesson of human life. Life is not rightly conceived as terminating in the grave. Death interrupts not the continuity of existence. The faculties of human nature, so far as they are immaterial, are projected at death into a new and ample sphere. We shall enter that sphere with the attainments and graces of this life, only without the limitations to which this life is necessarily subject. We shall reap as we have sown. "That which makes the question concerning a future life to be of so great importance to us," says Bishop Butler, "is our capacity of happiness and misery. And that which makes the consideration of it to be of so great importance to us, is the supposition of our happiness and misery hereafter depending upon our actions here."[1]

Let me sum up the conclusions of this chapter.

We have seen that Immortality as a doctrine has not always and everywhere borne the same meaning.

It cannot be rightly understood except by a study of human nature in its elements or parts.

Human nature consists not of body and the bodily powers alone, but of the vital principle, the desire, the affection, the reason and the spirit.

All that is not body, when set against the body, is the soul.

The distinction between soul and body is important as affecting the fact of Immortality.

[1] *Analogy*, part i. chap. ii. p. 33.

The distinction between the spirit and the other parts of the soul is important as affecting the nature of Immortality.

The soul which lives after death is not only spiritual but emotional and rational. It is the whole immaterial part of Man. It survives and survives eternally in the fulness of its intellectual, moral, and spiritual powers.

And its fate in the future life is in some manner—which will be presently investigated—fixed or conditioned by its character and discipline in this life.

CHAPTER II

HISTORY OF THE BELIEF

THE prevalent doctrine of Immortality has been largely determined by the Hebrew and Christian Scriptures of the Old and New Testaments. But it is a belief which reaches beyond and behind those Scriptures. It is one of those world-thoughts (if they may be so called) which are not of one place or time, but of all places and all times, and may be said to be the common heritage of mankind.

"Ut deos esse natura opinamur," says Cicero, "qualesque sint ratione cognoscimus, sic permanere animos arbitramur consensu omnium nationum."[1]

Modern research has been largely successful in tracing the phenomena of human life and thought

---

[1] "As it is by nature that we believe in the being of the Gods and by reason that we apprehend their nature, so it is by the unanimous opinion of all nations that we hold the doctrine of the permanent existence of the soul."—*Tusc. Disp.*, i., 16, 36.

back to their origin. It has laid bare the beginnings of things. The sciences of Anatomy and Embryology have demonstrated the close connexion between the human and even the lowest animal forms. Comparative Philology has revealed, by the intimate study of language, national and social relations which were scarcely imagined a century ago; it has followed the many diverging currents of human speech to their source. Comparative Mythology has shown the evolution of refined and disciplined beliefs from a few crude and simple apprehensions. Sociology has discovered the germs of modern institutions in the usages of primitive society. Everywhere it is the sense of history—the sense of development—which is men's guide in judging the present by the past.

But while primitive ideas, beliefs and usages have been thus brought prominently into light, the actual speculative value which belongs to them has been often forgotten or misunderstood. Some time ago their importance was minimised; it is now apt to be exaggerated. For instance, the Darwinian theory, establishing the descent of man, or the possibility of his descent, from a lower form of animal life, has been taken in a sense to fetter his capacity for the development of spiritual powers. But nothing in the past of man can cripple his present or his future. Man is what he is, and he will be what he will be; he is not, nor will he be, merely what he was. However lowly his origin may have been, even if he were made, as the Scripture tells, of the dust of the ground, there can be no limitation of his possible greatness. In the Divine view the end is prior to the beginning. The early beliefs which human history exhibits are not complete or absolute; they are promises of better things; they are the germs out of which new and great beliefs will some day grow; they are the steps of the ladder by which man climbs to his splendid destiny, and the ladder, though it is set up on earth, ascends to Heaven.

The belief in God is itself an instance of this law. History does not exhibit this belief as fully realised in the dawn of human society; it has been doubted if the belief exists then at all. Monotheism is not the basis of religious thought, but its climax. In the history of belief man ascends from many gods to one God, or, indeed, from many powers, physical and animate, but not Divine, to Polytheism, and so to the worship of the one true God. Beyond that worship, beyond that belief, it is impossible to rise. It is felt to be true because it is final. To it all prior beliefs and speculations tend. From it issue the consequent beliefs which sanctify life. There is a slow but sure consolidation of belief regarding the Divine Nature, and it assumes the permanent form of a belief in the one God.

It is so too with the doctrine of the human soul. The belief in the soul—in its reality, its continuous existence, its supreme value—is not an initial but a final belief of Humanity. It is the highest article of the highest Faith. No more than the germ—the primordial spring—of this great belief is discernible in the early movements of the human intellect and conscience. But it is beliefs which are germinal that elevate human nature; the revelations of God are never complete, they are gradual and progressive, and it is "at sundry times and in divers manners," *i.e.*, in many parts and in many modes, that He unfolds the truths which men most need to know.

To argue that the truth of Divine things is more likely to reside in the feelings and imaginations of savage races than in the sustained and reasoned convictions of civilised society is to read history backwards; it is to argue that infancy is wiser than maturity, and that the child knows more of his Maker than the full-grown man. Belief, like civilisation, is a development, it advances by steps; and every step is won slowly and even painfully, but the last stage is truer than the first. All that may be justly said of human nature is that the first faint germ of belief, no less than its full flower, is a witness to the native intuitions of the heart.

It is not true that Man believes, always and everywhere, in the one God. But it is true that everywhere, when man attains to a certain stage of intellectual and moral progress, he developes or tends to develope a belief in one God. That belief is the crown of all preceding beliefs. They point or converge towards it. And beyond it they cannot reach. Monotheism is, as it were, the resting-place of the human soul after many questionings and many strivings through long ages.

Similarly it is not true that Man at all stages of his history has logically realised or expressed the doctrine of the soul, although it has lain, as a seed, within his conscience. But it is true that Man, as he advances in thought and culture, becomes more and more inspired with a conviction of the soul's proper being and character and destiny. The higher his civilisation, the greater is the value which he sets upon the soul, whether in itself or in its relation to the body. And the teaching of Jesus Christ in regard to the soul is as far in advance of all other religious teachings as is His morality of other moralities or His Person of the persons of all who in human history have been the founders and exponents of other religions than the Christian.

Thus it appears that the belief in the existence and dignity of the soul is as it were the focus in which other beliefs, simpler and more primitive, are found to unite.

The object of this chapter is to trace the progress of religious thought respecting the soul until it reaches its climax in the Gospel of Christ. Such a survey of beliefs can be but imperfect; but it may perhaps not be inadequate to its purpose.

The primitive beliefs of men assume or tend to assume the form which by Dr. Tylor and others after him has been termed Animism.

Animism is the sense of universal personality. It was natural that man should realise in himself the fact of personality. It was not less natural that he should ascribe to all animate beings, and in a measure even to inanimate things, the personality of which he was conscious in himself. And it was natural, or not unnatural, that he should distinguish the personality so completely from the matter or vesture in which it was contained as to imagine that the two could be divorced without any necessary destruction or injury of the person.

Animism, then, is the first philosophical, as well as the first religious, theory of life.

From it arose the impersonation of natural objects, Man saw not fountains only, but the goddesses of fountains, or Naiads; not woods only, but the nymphs of the woods, or Dryads. He lived in an invisible fairy-land; nay, he could often persuade himself that he beheld in valley or forest, or on the green grass of the moorland, the evident traces of the fairy-forms in which he believed. The world seemed richer then and brighter to all men than it has seemed since; but of all men it seemed richest and brightest to the Greeks.

Hence arose, too, in human minds the belief in the ghosts or spirits of the dead, a belief to which the consciousness of dreams may well have given probability and effect. And although the belief in human spirits as manifesting themselves after death has been much discredited by folly and imposture, yet from its strength and universality it deserves respect as attesting a powerful intuitive conviction of Humanity.

And hence arose in human minds the consciousness of something more precious, because more permanent, than the body, a reality underlying the phenomena of personal experience, and of that something as being essentially the man.

From the primary intuitions or imaginations of Animism to the Christian conception and cultivation of the soul, as transcendently superior to the body, the process of thought is simple, constant and inevitable. The great belief once sown in the field of human conscience springs up and bears its natural fruit.

But this belief, as has been said, is independent of Christianity or any supposed Divine Revelation. It is found not only among such peoples as have considered themselves to be in one sense or other the favourites of Heaven, but among peoples who did not understand it and could give no account of it, but regarded it as a natural self-evident truth. Neither Judaism nor Christianity originated it; they did but accept it as pre-existent and modify or expand it.

Literature is in its nature no sufficient witness to the beliefs of an uncivilised and unlettered society. Yet as soon as human thought began to express itself in writing, one of its most frequent expressions was the belief in the soul's Immortality. A few passages chosen for their typical significance will illustrate the widespread character of the belief.

Upon its existence among primitive races it will be sufficient to quote the statements made, as the results of prolonged inquiry, by authorities so distinguished as M. Renouf and Dr. Tylor. Of these the former says:—"A belief in the persistence of life after death, and the observation of religious practices founded upon the belief, may be discovered in every part of the world, in every age, and among men representing every degree and variety of culture." [1]

The latter:—" Looking at the religion of the lower races as a whole, we shall at least not be ill-advised in taking as one of its general and principal elements the doctrine of the soul's future life." [2]

Mr. Alger, then, is not wrong in his conclusion, " The belief of mankind that a soul or ghost survives the body has been so nearly universal as to appear like the spontaneous result of an instinct." [3]

Literature from its birth attests the belief in the survival of the soul after death, or its Immortality.

---

[1] *Hibbert Lectures*, p. 124. [2] *Primitive Culture*, vol. ii. p. 21.
[3] *A Critical History of the Doctrine of a Future Life*, p. 583.

Thus Bunsen, following Professor Max Müller, quotes, as from the Vedas, such passages as these:—

1. An address to the spirit of the dead, when the funeral pile is lighted:

> "Depart, depart, along these ancient paths,
> By which our fathers have gone home to rest;
> The God Varuna shalt thou now behold
> And Yama, the two kings who take our gifts.
> Go to the fathers, sojourn there with Yama
> In highest heaven, fit meed of thy deserts,
> Leave there all evil, then go home once more,
> And take a form of radiant glory bright. . . .
> There where the pious dwell, and roam in peace,
> Shall God Sàvitri bear thee to their ranks."[1]

2. An appeal to Soma in the hymn of Kasyapa:

> "To the world where unfading Light, where Sunshine itself hath its home,
> Thither bring me, O Soma, where no harm and no death ever come;
> Where Yama as sovereign rules, where the innermost heaven exists,
> Where the great waters repose, oh, there let me dwell an immortal!
> In the heavenly vaults where man lives and moves at his pleasure,
> Where are the mansions of light, oh, there let me dwell an immortal!
> Where wishes and longing abide, where the sun ever beams in his glory,
> Where bliss that can satisfy dwells, oh, there let me dwell, an immortal!

---

[1] *God in History*, vol. i. p. 310, Winkworth's Translation.

Where gladness and joy may be found, where pleasure and rapture prevail,
Where every wish is fulfilled, oh, there let me dwell an immortal!"[1]

But even more striking is the noble passage of the *Bhagavadgítá* where the Deity is represented as saying of men slain in battle :

"You have grieved for those who deserve no grief, and you talk words of wisdom. Learned men grieve not for the living nor the dead. Never did I not exist, nor you, nor these rulers of men ; nor will any one of us ever hereafter cease to be. . . . These bodies appertaining to the embodied (self) which is eternal, indestructible, and indefinable, are said to be perishable ; therefore do engage in battle, O descendant of Bharata ! He who thinks it to be the killer and he who thinks it to be the killed, both know nothing. It kills not, is not killed. It is not born, nor does it ever die, nor, having existed, does it exist no more. Unborn, everlasting, unchangeable, and primeval, it is not killed when the body is killed. O son of Prithâ ! how can that man who knows it thus to be indestructible, everlasting, unborn, and inexhaustible, how and whom can he kill, whom can he cause to be killed ? As a man, casting off old

[1] *God in History*, vol. i. p. 314.

clothes, puts on others and new ones, so the embodied (self) casting off old bodies, goes to others and new ones. Weapons do not divide it (into pieces); fire does not burn it; waters do not moisten it; the wind does not dry it up. It is not divisible; it is not combustible; it is not to be moistened; it is not to be dried up. It is everlasting, all-pervading, staple, firm, and eternal."[1]

But a passage of still more venerable antiquity occurs in the Katha-Upanishad, which is an allegory of a sage who descended into the invisible world to wrest the secret of existence from Death:

"Beyond the senses is the mind, beyond the mind is the highest (created) Being, higher than that Being is the Great Self, higher than the Great, the highest Undeveloped.

"Beyond the Undeveloped is the Person, the all-pervading and entirely imperceptible. Every creature that knows him is liberated, and obtains Immortality.

"His form is not to be seen, no one beholds him with the eye. He is imagined by the heart, by wisdom, by the mind. Those who know this, are immortal.

"When the five instruments of knowledge stand

[1] *Sacred Books of the East*, vol. viii. pp. 43, 44.

still together with the mind, and when the intellect does not move, that is called the highest state.

"This, the firm holding back of the senses, is what is called Yoga. He must be free from thoughtlessness then, for Yoga comes and goes.

"He (the Self) cannot be reached by speech, by mind, or by the eye. How can it be apprehended except by him who says : 'He is'?

"By the words 'He is,' is he to be apprehended, and by (admitting) the reality of both (the invisible Brahman and the visible world, as coming from Brahman). When he has been apprehended by the words 'He is,' then his reality reveals itself.

"When all desires that dwell in his heart cease, then the mortal becomes immortal, and obtains Brahman.

"When all the ties of the heart are severed here on earth, then the mortal becomes immortal—here ends the teaching."[1]

It is not my purpose, nor am I competent, to examine the theology of the Vedic hymns, ranging as they do perhaps over a period of a thousand years; I am only concerned to show that they

---

[1] *Sacred Books of the East*, vol. xv. pp. 22, 23. I owe this reference to the kindness of Professor Cowell.

contain and express the hope of personal existence after death, of Immortality.

The same hope asserts itself, though with numerous variations, in the religious systems (so far as they are ascertainable) of the Accadians and after them of the Babylonians and Assyrians, of the Persians, of the Egyptians, whose influence upon Jewish thought will be presently considered, and of the Greeks. In them all it is interesting to observe how the idea of the future life was gradually purified, gradually spiritualised. Of the Babylonians, for instance, Professor Sayce says that their Hades "closely resembles the Hades of the Homeric poems;" it is "a land of forgetfulness and of darkness, where the good and evil deeds of this life are remembered no more." But he adds: "Side by side with this pitiful picture of the world beyond the grave, there were the beginnings of higher and nobler ideas. . . . Little by little, as the conception of the gods and their dwelling-place became spiritualised, the conception of the future condition of mankind became spiritualised also. The condition of the Immortality of the conscious soul began to dawn upon the Babylonian mind, and along with it necessarily went the doctrine of rewards and punishments for the actions committed in the flesh."[1]

For the teaching of the Zend-Avesta in its highest form it is enough to refer to the striking passage in which it is told how the soul of the righteous and the soul of the wicked quit the body at death, and each of them after three days meets its own conscience, the one as a beauteous maid, the other as a foul old woman, and the one passes through the three paradises of Good-Thought, Good-Word and Good-Deed to the celestial bliss, and the other through the three hells of Evil-Thought, Evil-Word and Evil-Deed to the infernal misery.[2]

And these quotations, so significant of a hope in things unseen, may end with some lines of the most religious of the Greek poets, the poet Pindar. For he too had caught a vision of reward and penalty waiting upon the deeds of earth, and he sang how " the guilty souls no sooner die than they pay the penalty of their sin, and one there is who judgeth beneath the earth the evil deeds wrought within the realm of Zeus and doth pronounce sentence under a compulsion that he loathes ; but the good dwell for

[1] *Hibbert Lectures*, v. pp. 364, 365.
[2] *Sacred Books of the East*, vol. xxiii. pp. 314 *sqq*.

ever in the light of the sun, alike by day and by night, and are the inheritors of an unlaborious life, they vex not the earth with strength of arm nor the waters of the sea all through their days, but as many as were gladly true to their plighted word pass a tearless time among the honoured of the gods ; the others endure trouble too piteous to look upon." [1]

For enough has now been said to demonstrate the reality and universality of the hope of a life transcending the grave.

It is well known that to this rising and spreading tide of belief in a life of the soul, distinct from the physical life and transcending and surviving it, there is one remarkable exception. Just where the belief might have been expected to be strongest, it fails. The early books of the Old Testament afford, it is said, no traces of a belief in the soul's Immortality.

The strangeness of this fact demands consideration.

The Jews, as a people, were inspired with a strong and vital feeling for religion. The constant assertion of that feeling was the great service which Judaism rendered to Humanity. The Jews had always many faults ; they were narrow, isolated, and

[1] *Olympian Odes*, ii. 57 *sqq.*

self-centred ; they were deficient in many of the powers and graces of their neighbours ; they were not distinguished in arms or in arts ; they were unpopular, and the secular world looked down upon them as a prey ; yet their religious literature has occupied, and occupies still, an unrivalled place in the affections and interests of mankind. They possessed what may be called a genius for religion. They were in the realm of faith supreme authorities, as in the realm of art were the Greeks, and in the realm of politics the Romans. No disappointment, no disaster could injure the supremacy of the religious sentiment among the Jews. It centred all through their history in that Messianic hope which has been the great centripetal force of Judaism in all ages and among all nations of the world. Yet it is in this people, the most religious people among men, that the hope of the Immortal Life—the hope most deeply characteristic of religion —was for many centuries practically non-existent. How is it possible to account for this fact ?

It is perhaps hardly necessary at this present day to consider in detail the paradoxical explanation of Bishop Warburton. His argument, advanced with much dialectical ingenuity and with a vast display of learning in the *Divine Legation of Moses*, is briefly this : that a religion invented by Man could not have failed to assume a life beyond the grave as one of its cardinal tenets, that the Mosaic Law makes no such assumption, that it could not therefore be the invention of Man, and that, not being the invention of Man, it must have been the revelation of God.

To quote his own words : "If religion be necessary to civil Government, and if religion cannot subsist under the common dispensation of Providence without a future state of rewards or punishments ; so consummate a lawgiver (as Moses) would never have neglected to inculcate the belief of such a state, had he not been well assured that an extraordinary Providence was indeed to be administered over his people : or were it possible he had been so infatuated, the impotency of a religion wanting a future state must very soon have concluded in the destruction of his Republic. Yet nevertheless it flourished and continued sovereign for many ages. These two proofs of the proposition (that an extraordinary Providence was really administered) drawn from the thing omitted and the person omitting, may be reduced to the following syllogisms :

"1. Whatsoever religion and society have no future state for their support, must be supported by an extraordinary Providence.

"The Jewish religion and society had no future state for their support.

"Therefore the Jewish religion and society were supported by an extraordinary Providence.

"And again :

"2. The ancient lawgivers universally believed that a religion without a future state could be supported only by an extraordinary Providence.

"Moses, an ancient lawgiver, learned in all the wisdom of the Egyptians (the principal part of which wisdom was inculcating the doctrine of a future life) instituted such a religion.

"Therefore Moses believed that his religion was supported by an extraordinary Providence."[1]

The argument is a paradox, and little more; still it rests upon a singular phenomenon. In all, or nearly all, religious literature, except the Mosaic, the belief in God and the belief in the soul's Immortality however erroneously held, are inextricably blended

[1] *The Divine Legation of Moses Demonstrated*, book vi., section vi., vol. iii., p. 241.

together. In the Mosaic Law the belief in God is strongest, the belief in Immortality is weakest. This is a fact that needs to be explained.

It appears to me that whatever explanation is offered must take account of the special character attaching to the early books of the Old Testament. In primitive society, not among the Jews only, but everywhere, the individual is of slight importance; it is the race—the tribe—the family which is everything. The individual can hardly be said to enjoy a personal existence, or at least a personal moral existence, in himself. It is not the individual who holds property. It is not the individual who conducts business. It is not the individual who sins or who is punished for sinning. "The moral elevation and moral debasement of the individual appear to be confounded with, or postponed to, the merits and offences of the group to which the individual belongs. If the community sins, its guilt is much more than the sum of the offences committed by its members; the crime is a corporate act, and extends in its consequences to many more persons than have shared in its actual perpetration. If, on the other hand, the individual is conspicuously guilty, it is his children, his kinsfolk, his tribesmen, or his fellow-citizens who suffer with him, and sometimes for him."[1]

Society, in fact, begins with collectivism, in whatever sense or degree the collectivism may be understood; it does not begin with individualism. The individual is regarded as a member of a body; he is not regarded in himself.

The second commandment of the Decalogue is a witness to the Jewish sense of corporate or collective responsibility for the actions of the individual. It is strange that Christians should so often hear and read that commandment without appreciating either its close affinity to the teachings of modern science upon heredity, or its wide departure from the code of current Christian morals. But it is enough to say now that the moral consequences of actions are represented in it as collective and not as individual. "I the Lord thy God visit the sins of the fathers upon the children unto the third and fourth generation of them that hate Me, and show mercy unto thousands in them that love Me and keep My commandments." Such moral teaching is accepted as natural throughout the Pentateuchal literature. It marks a stage in the history of human thought

[1] Sir Henry Maine, *Ancient Law*, chap. v. p. 127.

—a stage where the individual is worth little, and the body of which he is a member is supreme. Collectivism then, and not individualism, is the keynote of the moral teaching in the Pentateuch.

But if the individual counted for little in this life, it was not to be expected that he would count for more in the next. Personality, thrown into the shade, as it was, in this world could not well be projected into another world. Therefore it was that the same difficulty which in pagan nations and among pagan thinkers of acute and enlightened intellectuality, as among the Greeks, obscured the doctrine of an absolute Immortal Life—the difficulty of conceiving personality—told among the Jews against the belief that the soul of each individual would survive in simple personal existence after death.

There is another thought which throws light upon the attitude of the early Hebrew Scriptures towards Immortality. What is the great conception which these Scriptures keep in view ? It is not the privilege or destiny of the individual, it is the institution of a Divine society upon earth. The Messianic idea, as has been said, pervades the Old Testament; but the idea of the Messiah was not originally, or principally, that he would be the Saviour of individual souls, it was rather that he would be the Founder of a Kingdom. The Gospels in the New Testament show clearly enough that the contemporaries of our Lord's life not only conceived of the Messianic Kingdom as a deliverance from thraldom, or in other words as the creation of a new secular Theocracy, but were impatient and intolerant of any other conception than this. But it was the object of the Mosaic law to foster and cultivate the idea of a Divine Kingdom on earth. For this the ritual of Judaism was a preparation ; of this it was a type and an exponent.

"The conception of a perfect kingdom," says Dorner,[1] "overpowers that of personality." The Old Testament is the history of an elect people, but not of elect persons. Thus it is that in the Scriptures of the Old Testament the fate of the individual, whether it be present or future, does not come frequently or directly into question. It matters little what happens to the individual, so that the Divine Kingdom is set up in the world. Apart from the spiritual or religious aspect of life, the case of Greek thought is not dissimilar to that of Hebrew. In the

[1] *System of Christian Doctrine*, vol. ii. p. 85, in Clark's Foreign Theological Library.

writings of Plato and Aristotle as much as in the Law of Moses the individual is merged in the society of which he is a member. The duty of the State to the individual is scarcely considered. That the State exists for the good of the citizens who compose it, if it be a truism in the modern world, would in the ancient have seemed a paradox. But the duty of the individual to the State is paramount. It is the State which invests his life with meaning and dignity; to the State, therefore, he owes not his life only but, if the demand is made of him, all that constitutes life a boon. Thus Ethics is itself, as Aristotle says, a branch of Politics. There is no morality but such as is relative to the needs and capacities of the State. It would not have occurred to the ancient Greek philosopher to inquire if the individual life withered or flourished, so long as the State was secure. Nor did it occur to the ancient Hebrew legislator to discuss the fate of the individual either in this life or in the next, when his heart was bent upon establishing and ennobling the Divine Kingdom in the world of men.

If this is a just interpretation of the Mosaic law, it follows that the absence of the soul's Immortality, as a doctrine regulating man's conception of the universe and of his own relation to the present and the future, is not an evidence, any more than it is a disproof, of Divine inspiration; it is the natural outcome of circumstances. That the circumstances were special and transitory may be admitted; but they could not have been other than they were. Spiritual individualism, although foreshadowed in several passages of prophetical and still more of apocryphal literature, is the revelation of Jesus Christ.

The Jews learnt much about the soul in the course of centuries; but they did not learn the two great truths, that all human souls are of equal value and that the value of each soul is supreme.

Again, it is necessary to remember that the Mosaic law was in some sense an inevitable reaction against the creed and ritual of Egypt. When "Israel came out of Egypt," they came with deeply imprinted memories of oppression. Except, indeed, in certain few rebellious hours, of which the Pentateuch speaks with a solemnity approximating to horror, they cast the beliefs and symbols of the Egyptian religious system behind their backs. It was because the episode of the Golden Calf was a return to the life which symbolised for the Jews a state of spiritual darkness that it awoke sentiments of indignation and severity in the heart of Moses. For the deliverance from Egypt was a type of the soul's deliverance from ignominy and sin.

What, then, was the striking feature of Egyptian life? It was religion. But not only so, it was a religion in which the present was enveloped in the future and life was overshadowed by death. A living writer says: " The Egyptian lived among tombs whose size and splendour reduced into insignificance the dwellings of the living, and the most characteristic features of his mythology were representations of the death and resurrection of nature in winter and summer, as types representing the death and resurrection of man."[1]

The story of ancient Egypt is a warning of the paralysis that may creep over the beneficent activities of the religious spirit, when it is used to divert men's thoughts from the things of sight to the unseen world. For religion is the aspiration of the human soul to God; but it ceases to be true religion, if it loses the sense either of Heaven or of earth. The Egyptians of old dwelt in their minds and consciences upon the life beyond the grave; their reflective habit solemnised and elevated their lives,

[1] Caird, *Evolution of Religion*, vol. i. p. 32.

but it sterilised them. The shadow of futurity rested, as a cloud, upon the present. They thought not how to live, but how to survive death. The striking edifices of Egypt were tombs, and to-day the ancient homes of the living have long since mouldered in decay, but the tombs and the sepulchral monuments remain. The pyramids of Ghizeh and Sakhara are undying witnesses to death.

The effect of Egypt as it now is upon the mind of a traveller who visits it from the West is probably less uniform and therefore less impressive than it was in antiquity. To-day a stir of life pulses through the veins and arteries of that mysterious country. Egypt is felt to have a future as well as a past. But during the centuries of Egyptian history to which the pyramids afford an immortal attestation, the sense of a never-ceasing, never-ending struggle against the power of death—a struggle carried on with the accumulated resources of human labour, human skill and human devotion—must have seemed, as indeed it was, supreme.

It was upon death and upon the fate of the soul after death that the thoughts of the Egyptian priests and people brooded perpetually. They evolved a positive complete theory of the future life. The

Book of the Dead is at once an eschatology and a ritual of the dead. And here it may be permitted me to quote the words of Professor Salmond: "The idea of a future judgment for all men was a cardinal point in the Egyptian conception of a future life. This made it a distinctly moral conception. The soul, which seems to have been thought of as coming from the gods, had a retributive future before it. It was for Osiris or for Set[1] on earth, and its deeds here decided its future. Osiris was the judge. Everything turned upon his judgment. The justified one was identified with him, received his name, enjoyed his protection and guidance, and became himself an Osiris. When the dead man reaches the Hall of the Double Truth, he is before the throne of this Divine judge. The goddess Maāt, the goddess of Justice, Truth, or Law, is there, holding a sceptre and the symbol of life. The scales are set; the man's heart in the one, the image of Maāt in the other. Horus watches the index. Thoth or Tehati, the god of letters, takes the record. The standard of judgment is high. It covers all the great requirements of truth,

[1] Set was, in the Egyptian mythology, the principle of evil, as Osiris was of good.

purity, righteousness, charity, piety. Above the balance are the forty-two assessors, whose office is with the forty-two great forms of sin. The departed makes his confession. It takes the form of a negative statement, denying his guilt in respect of these sins. His conscience, or moral nature, symbolised by the heart in the scale, speaks for him. If the judgment is favourable, he regains the use of hands, limbs and mind; he receives back what he had lost by death. His soul, his Kâ, his shadow are restored, and he begins a new life. If the judgment is unfavourable, he bears the penalty of loss and pain."[1]

Much more is there in the *Book of the Dead* respecting the discipline of the justified soul for its full and final blessing; but it lies beyond the scope of this essay. For I am seeking to delineate, however briefly, the general progress of the belief in the invisible future life; I am not writing a history of Egyptian beliefs.

But the special Egyptian belief concerning the dead is emphasised in the many poetic symbols and images with which the life of ancient Egypt was replete. The serpent, the scarabæus, the butterfly,

---

[1] *The Christian Doctrine of Immortality*, chap. iv. p. 59.

are all suggestive of the soul's emancipation from the prison of the body into a new Immortal Life. And everywhere the death and resurrection of nature—the death in winter, the resurrection in the springtide—typified as they are by the loss and the finding of Osiris, appear as emblems of Man's death, and of his resurrection after death into Immortality.

Thus the Jews had in Egypt been the witnesses of a religious system in which the creed and ritual of a dominant hierarchy pervaded and regulated human life. The Egyptians passed their days under the shadow of religion, and their present was insensibly darkened by the thought of the unknown and awful future.

It may well be believed, then, that the great Legislator under whose guidance the Exodus of the Jewish people from Egypt took place, desired in the interest of true religion to break with the religious beliefs and practices of Egyptian society. The breach so made by the Mosaic law was complete and irreparable. If the Egyptians worshipped many gods, the Israelites were to "have none other God" than Jehovah. If the Egyptians employed innumerable forms and idols as symbolising the various aspects of the Divine Nature, the Israelites were cautioned against "making any graven image." If the Egyptians sought to immortalise their mighty dead by monuments that should endure as long as time, the leaders and reformers of Hebrew society were "gathered to their fathers" without any pageant of religious ceremonial. And if the Egyptians brooded over the fate of the dead, if they diversified it with an elaboration of pictorial art and fancy and invested it with the solemn mystery of judgment, the Israelites must find their hopes and gratifications and the practical sanctions of their morality within the confines of the present life.

It was not irreligion then, but the strength of the religious feeling, that confined the beliefs and speculations of the Jewish people after the Exodus to the present life. The theology of the Pentateuch is a reaction against the superstition of the Egyptian hierarchy. It would seem to me that the Mosaic secularism (if it may be called so), *i.e.*, the limitation of the religious view to the present life, is in some senses a parallel to the Buddhist doctrine of Nirvana; for obscure as that doctrine is and various as are the interpretations which have been given of it, it may, I think, be most reasonably regarded as a reaction against the composite imaginations which had gathered in the successive phases of Brahminical religion around the life of Man beyond the grave. In the one case the human mind found a refuge in the disregard of the future spiritual existence, and in the other it found a refuge in the conception of a future existence calm, passionless, and all but dead.

But whether this be so or not, it is safe to assert that the Jews, being under the Mosaic law, put aside to a large extent the thought of the future, because they were unwilling that the future, with its sombre gloom, should overshadow the practical immediate duties of the present. Their present-worldliness (so to speak of it), was a protest against the Egyptian other-worldliness. It was a protest not only of logical necessity, but of definite moral elevation.

The theology of the Pentateuch may be said to embody the first stage in the beliefs of the Jewish nation touching Immortality. The soul's Immortality was not declared, it was not denied; it was simply left out of sight.

Yet the Jews, like other nations, could not rest content with a mere indifference to the future life of the soul. They could not avoid the question, Is death the end of the soul's life? Does the soul indeed perish with the body?

The answer supplied by Jewish thought is the doctrine of Sheol.[1] It is the second stage in the belief of Immortality.

The word "Sheol" is the Hebrew equivalent of the Greek "Hades" and the Egyptian "Amenti." It is said to mean "the hollow place"; and, if so, it is exactly represented by the English word "hell," when used, as in the Creed, to denote the unseen world of spirits, and not, as too often in common phraseology, the place in which spirits are believed to undergo a ceaseless pain.

The Hebrew word Sheol, as is well known, is variously translated in the Authorised Version of the Bible; it is "hell," "the grave," "the pit," and so on. One of the signal services of the Revised Version is that it brings out the conception of Sheol into a clear and definite light.

Sheol, then, is the under-world, the world of spirits. Into it all men descend. "What man is he that shall live and not see death," says one of the Psalmists, "that shall deliver his soul from

[1] In the part of this essay which relates to the Hebrew Sheol, I have been much indebted to Professor Salmond's treatise on *The Christian Doctrine of Immortality*, book ii. chap. ii. pp. 198, *sqq.*

the power of Sheol?"[1] All the dead are there, the rich and the poor, the just and the unjust, the lord and his slaves, fathers and mothers, young men and maidens, and little children. In the Book of Proverbs it is told that Sheol is one of the four things that are "never satisfied," and "say not, It is enough."[2]

Sheol is contrasted with the upper world of light and life. It lies deep down in the bowels of the earth. It is "a land of darkness, as darkness itself; and of the shadow of death, without any order, and where the light is as darkness."[3] It is a land of silence and sadness and immortal sleep, a land in which the Almighty shows no marvels, and the soul wanders in a random life.

What or where Sheol is, the Scripture tells not, except in words as dubious as these. It is a place but not a place, a home but a home unwelcome, a mere negation of all that makes life sweet and dear.

Yet into it, as has been said, all men descend at death. There is no difference. Manifold as is the fate of the myriads of human beings in life, in Sheol it is one. The thought of a distinction among the dead, whether it be due to rank or

[1] Psalm lxxxix. 48. [2] Proverbs xxx. 15, 16. [3] Job x. 22.

character in the present life, is foreign to the Hebrew conception of Sheol. The good and the evil, the happy and the miserable, are alike there. A life unending and unbroken—a life which is but as the shadow of the present—awaits them all. All go unto one place; for all there is one fate.

It is not impossible to deduce from the words of Holy Scripture some idea, though faint and feeble, of the life imagined in Sheol. When the spirit is said to go down into Sheol, it is the man's personality which survives. But it is his personality alone. He is the same man, but he is no more the man endowed with his proper faculties of will, emotion, intellect and conscience. He is but the shadow of himself, as his life is no longer real and actual, but shadowy. He is the same man; for others can recognise him, and he them, in the world of spirits; but all that gives strength and purpose to life is gone from him. No words can describe the vacuity of the life in Sheol better than some of the Preacher, Koheleth or Ecclesiastes: "The living know that they shall die: but the dead know not anything, neither have they any more a reward, for the memory of them is forgotten. Also their love, and their hatred, and their envy is now perished ; neither have they any more a portion for ever in anything that is done under the sun. . . . Whatsoever thy hand findeth to do, do it with thy might, for there is no work, nor device, nor knowledge, nor wisdom in Sheol, whither thou goest."[1]

As in the Homeric Hades, so too in the Scriptural Sheol the loss of human interests and associations is acutely regretted. That such a life should be worth living in comparison with the life of earth is a thought which does not enter the mind of the heathen poet or the Hebrew Psalmist. They who live in Sheol are, as it were, but shadowy kings on shadowy thrones, men who have lost the pleasure of knowledge, the capacity and even the memory of friendship, the hope and desire of better things. They can no more learn or labour or be happy. They can but cast their eyes half-consciously backwards to their own past, and, remembering but imperfectly what it was, pray that their present should be even as the past.

But to the Hebrew poets and thinkers it was not the loss of human interests and associations that seemed the most painful deprivation. They believed

[1] Ecclesiastes ix. 5, 6, 10.

that the spirits in Sheol were cut off not only from Man, but from God. In Sheol there was no room for praise or prayer, no room for communion with the Eternal. It is difficult to over-estimate the pathos of such words as these, spoken by devout Jews to whom the presence of God was as life itself : "What profit is there in my blood, when I go down to the pit ? Shall the dust praise Thee ? Shall it declare Thy truth ?"[1] "In death there is no remembrance of Thee ; in Sheol who shall give Thee thanks ?"[2] "Shall Thy lovingkindness be declared in the grave ? or Thy faithfulness in destruction ? Shall Thy wonders be known in the dark ? and Thy righteousness in the land of forgetfulness ?"[3] "Sheol cannot praise Thee ; death cannot celebrate Thee ; they that go down into the pit cannot hope for Thy truth."[4]

These words are enough, though it were easy to multiply them, and they prove that the most devout and spiritually-minded Jews looked forward to Sheol as a place which none could escape, and yet which none could enter without a mournful sinking of heart. Sorrow, failure, weariness, despondency—

[1] Psalm xxx. 9.
[2] Psalm vi. 5.
[3] Psalm lxxxviii. 11, 12.
[4] Isaiah xxxviii. 18.

these are the thoughts suggested by Sheol. And, still more, when the spirit of a man went down to Sheol, it abandoned the hope of a better life. The destiny of Sheol was universal, and it was eternal. None might escape going down into it, and none that went down might return. In it the highest and the lowest of mankind, the saints and the sinners, those whose lives had been the blessings and those whose lives had been the curses of the world, were alike, and alike eternally. In the mournful words of the patriarch Job, "As the cloud is consumed and vanisheth away; so he that goeth down to Sheol shall come up no more."[1]

Such was the second stage of Jewish belief touching the future of the soul; it was the second, but it could not be final.

The belief in Sheol is a denial of the soul's extinction, it is an assertion of the soul's existence after death; but it possesses no element of the moralising, sanctifying associations, no satisfaction of the hopes and yearnings and aspirations which cluster and, so long as human nature remains unchanged, will cluster still around the creed of Immortality.

[1] Job vii. 9.

There is a third stage, not altogether clearly defined, in Hebrew theology.

That theology had rejected the idea of annihilation and had so created the belief in Sheol; but in process of time it rejected the idea of Sheol as the receptacle of all the spirits of men. In both cases the process was moral rather than intellectual.

To the student of the Old Testament, if he stops short of the prophetical books, it becomes clear that the early Hebrew writers, having limited their religious conceptions to the present world, were often at a loss for the means of reconciling the Divine justice with the actual conditions and dispensations of human life. The simple theory of the Pentateuch that temporal felicity is the reward of temporal virtue broke down. The Book of Job —perhaps the earliest book in the Bible—is itself a protest against that theory; for every reader of the book must feel that the restoration of Job to all and more than all his temporal blessings in the last chapter is at the best an inadequate solution of the problem with which the book attempts to deal. But it is in the Psalms that the sense of an unsolved mystery in human life assumes the most definite form. One of the Psalmists confesses in touching language how the mystery puzzled and distressed him, and how insoluble it seemed, until he went into the sanctuary of God, though even there the solution which occurred to him was only the assurance that the punishment of sin, however long it may be delayed, is actually accomplished in the present life. "Until I went," he says, "into the sanctuary of God, then understood I their end. Surely thou didst set them (the wicked) in slippery places; thou castedst them down into destruction. How are they brought into desolation, as in a moment! they are utterly consumed with terrors. As a dream when one awaketh, so, O Lord, when Thou awakest, Thou shalt despise their image."[1]

But the facts of life are positive; and they tell so strongly against the present necessary connexion of moral virtue and temporal success that the thoughts of men were inevitably drawn beyond the limits of the present world, and in proportion as the moral contradictions of life pressed themselves upon the conscience, the belief in the soul's Immortality assumed a greater strength and solidity.

Thoughtful and devout men felt instinctively that religion demanded a life other and larger than the

[1] Psalm lxxiii. 17-20.

present. But Sheol was no satisfaction of that demand. For the two innate ideas which have in the course of human history rendered the belief in Immortality axiomatic are the longing of the spirit of man for continued existence and the desire of the conscience for a vindication of God's moral dealing with His children.

But the life of Sheol was too faint and shadowy, too near to death, to afford the sense of Immortality. And the life of Sheol, being in its nature the same for the good and the evil, left the moral problem of the conscience where it had been.

Thus the thinkers who in the later days of the monarchy tried to face the problem of life could not rest in the mere doctrine of the Sheol; they had taken one step, and they must take yet another. That step, as will be seen, was the conception of a spiritual and retributory Immortality.

It cannot be denied that in this case as in others the religious ideas of the Hebrew nation were at once quickened and purified by the painful experience of the Captivity. The effect of the Captivity in its influence upon Jewish thought and Jewish sentiment was profound. It finds no parallel, or finds it only in the effect produced by the capture and destruction of Jerusalem under Titus upon the mind of the early Christian Church. These great events were strong, cleansing moral forces.

The destruction of Jerusalem swept away the local or national limitations which might have fettered the free development of the Christian Church. The Captivity, by breaking the continuity of the Jewish national life, threw the thoughts of the devout Israelites back upon the relation of the individual soul to God. Thus it purified religion. It put an end to the idolatrous ritual which had come to be associated with the Monotheism of Israel. It awakened the sentiment of sacred personal responsibility as appears in such passages as that of Ezekiel : " The son shall not bear the iniquity of the father, neither shall the father bear the iniquity of the son ; the righteousness of the righteous shall be upon him, and the wickedness of the wicked shall be upon him."[1] Above all, it was the Captivity which led men to look for the Divine benediction, not in any national earthly prosperity, however great, but in that spiritual satisfaction which is the boon of all who, in any age or any land, repose their simple faith in God.

[1] Ezekiel xviii. 20.

Thus the conception of a personal Immortality rose before the eyes of men. It was the natural outcome of devout religious thought concentrating itself upon personal character and personal responsibility. The conception, it is true, had dawned upon men's eyes before the Captivity. It is enough to quote the wonderful words of the patriarch Job. "I know that my Redeemer liveth, and that He shall stand up at the last upon the earth: And after my skin hath been thus destroyed, yet from my flesh shall I see God; whom I shall see for myself, and mine eyes shall behold, and not another. My reins are consumed within me."[1] The translation is that of the Revisers of the Old Testament and, as so translated, the passage implies that for Job himself there is a Redeemer or a Vindicator; that Job shall die, but that his Redeemer shall live and live eternally; that though his skin shall wither and his flesh decay, yet shall Job behold his Redeemer, who is God; that he shall see Him with his own eyes, and, as it were, face to face, and his reins shall be consumed with the transport of the vision.

But it is in the Psalms and prophecies of the Exilic

[1] Job xix. 25-27.

or Post-exilic period that the faith in personal Immortality becomes most impressive. Let the following passages evince it :—

1. The 49th Psalm tells of the proud and impious men who trust in their riches as going down into the darkness of Sheol, but it tells also of a better fate laid up for the righteous. "Like sheep they are laid in Sheol." "Death shall feed on them . . . and their beauty shall consume in Sheol from their dwelling. But God will redeem my soul from the power of Sheol; for he shall receive me."[1]

2. The 73rd Psalm rises, like the 49th, to a higher thought than that of Sheol. "Nevertheless I am continually with Thee. Thou hast holden me by my right hand. Thou shalt guide me with Thy counsel, and afterward receive me to glory."[2]

3. Hosea's prophecy may be thought to contain the first idea, not of Immortality alone, but of Resurrection. "I will ransom them from the power of Sheol; I will redeem them from death: O death, I will be thy plagues; O Sheol, I will be thy destruction."[3] Such are his words, and they are echoed by St. Paul in the great chapter which Christian mourners know by heart.

[1] Psalm xlix. 14, 15. [2] Psalm lxxiii. 23, 24. [3] Hosea xiii. 14.

4. Ezekiel's vision [1] of the dry bones may perhaps be national rather than individual; it may typify the resurrection of a nation and not of its members. "Son of man," he writes, "these bones are the whole house of Israel." Yet it is difficult to believe that they who read of the breath coming from the four winds upon the bones that filled the valley until "they lived and stood up upon their feet, an exceeding great army," should have failed to catch the inspiration of a living personal Immortality.

5. Still stronger and more striking is the prophecy of Isaiah, designed to comfort the chosen people in their affliction. "Thy dead men shall live, together with my dead body shall they arise. Awake and sing, ye that dwell in dust; for thy dew is as the dew of herbs, and the earth shall cast out the dead." [2]

6. And this glowing hope—so sacred and sublime —which pervades the later canonical books of the Old Testament finds its consummation in the closing chapter of Daniel's prophecy. "But go thou thy way till the end be: for thou shalt rest, and stand in thy lot at the end of thy days." [3]

It were easy to pass from these passages to the teaching of our Lord in the Gospels. But between

---

[1] Ezekiel xxxvii. 1–14.   [2] Isaiah xxvi. 19.   [3] Daniel xii. 13.

the prophetical writings and the Gospels there is a link which is too frequently forgotten. That link is the Apocrypha.

It is one of the curious facts of ecclesiastical history, as Dr. Salmon has observed, that the action of the Council of Trent in placing the Apocrypha upon a level with the canonical writings of the Old and New Testament has led the Reformed Churches to disparage the Apocrypha. Yet the value of the Apocrypha is great as shedding light upon Jewish religious beliefs and hopes in the four centuries which lie between the close of the Old Testament Canon and the birth of our Lord, and upon none more than upon the faith in Immortality. "The Apocrypha," says Dr. Salmon,[1] "contains evidence that, in the later times to which it belongs, the doctrine of a future life had taken hold of the people as it had not done earlier. The third part of the Homily on the Fear of Death offers proofs of the belief in a future life held by 'the holy fathers of the old law,' but these proofs are taken exclusively from the Book of Wisdom. And it would not be possible to replace the two lessons for All Saints' Day by

[1] *Speaker's Commentary.* General Introduction to the Apocrypha, § 73.

two other Old Testament chapters expressing the same belief with equal distinctness."

The belief in Immortality is not always in the Apocrypha expressed with equal clearness and certainty, but it is there.

The following passages of the Book of Wisdom will show how strong the belief was and how greatly it had been developed. "God created man to be immortal, and made him to be an image of His own eternity."[1] "The souls of the righteous are in the hand of God, and there shall no torment touch them. In the sight of the unwise they seem to die, and their departure is taken for misery, and their going from us to be utter destruction; but they are in peace. For though they be punished in the sight of men, yet is their hope full of Immortality."[2] "The righteous live for evermore; their reward also is with the Lord, and the care of them is with the Most High."[3] "To know Thee is perfect righteousness: yea, to know Thy power is the root of Immortality."[4]

Along with these passages, which express a belief in Immortality as the reward of holy lives, others

---

[1] Wisdom of Solomon ii. 23.
[2] Ibid. iii. 1–4.
[3] Ibid. v. 15.
[4] Ibid. xv. 3.

occur, not always definite or consistent, but suggesting the doctrine of retribution for the wicked.

"They," *i.e.*, the unrighteous, "shall see him," *i.e.*, the wise, "and despise him; but God shall laugh them to scorn, and they shall hereafter be a vile carcase, and a reproach among the dead for evermore. . . . . And when they cast up the accounts of their sins, they shall come with fear, and their own iniquities shall convince them to their face."[1] "Over them only was spread an heavy night, an image of that darkness which should afterwards receive them: but yet were they unto themselves more grievous than the darkness."[2]

In the Book of Wisdom, then, appears the thought of a life surviving the grave, and of that life as containing in itself the reward of virtue and the penalty of sin. It is not uniformly or consistently maintained in the Apocrypha. It is strong in one book, as in the *Wisdom*, weak or fitful in another, as in *Ecclesiasticus*; at the most it is a hope or an aspiration rather than a faith; and it is only, as I think, in the Books of the Maccabees that the faith becomes definite and sure. The history of these books is not less inspiring than instructive. It

---

[1] Wisdom of Solomon iv. 18, 20.   [2] Ibid. xvii. 21.

is in the nature of a supreme national agony to elicit great thoughts and high aspirations. What the struggle of the Persian wars was to Æschylus and the struggle of the Reformation to Shakespeare, all that, and more than that, was the struggle against Antiochus Epiphanes to the contemporaries of the Maccabees. There is no occasion then for surprise that this should be the time when the thought of Immortality begins to dominate men's minds. Thus in the story of the seven brethren who were martyred and their mother occur these passages :—

"When he," the fourth son, "was ready to die, he said thus, It is good, being put to death by men, to look for hope from God to be raised up again by Him: as for thee"—he is addressing the king—"thou shalt have no resurrection to life."[1] And again in the story of Nicanor, "When as his blood was now quite gone, he plucked out his bowels, and taking them in both his hands he cast them upon the throng, and calling upon the Lord of life and spirit to restore him those again, he thus died."[2]

Passages such as these imply a faith not only in a spiritual life transcending the present, but indeed in a corporeal resurrection.

[1] 2 Maccabees vii. 14.   [2] Ibid. xiv. 46.

Thus the agony of the Maccabean struggle set the crown upon the Jewish desire for Immortality. That which had been a despair, then a dream, then a hope, then an aspiration became a fixed article of belief.

To sum up what has been said : By the time when the canon of the Old Testament closed in Malachi, or soon afterwards, and certainly before the coming of our Lord, the thought of the personal soul as endowed with Immortality had dawned as a vision of desire upon the hearts of the devout and religious Israelites. And not only so, but it was acknowledged that the soul, more than the body, more than the intellect, was the part of Man that was most closely related to his Maker. The soul would survive the body. It would inherit an eternal life. It would enter into the Divine Presence. It would attain the celestial beatitude. This was the thought which animated the Jews in their contests with their enemies, which gave them faith and courage and endurance, and which made them invincible, as all nations have been invincible when the certainty of the Divine protecting grace has possessed their minds.

The Jewish world then at the coming of our Lord stood, as it were, prepared for His teaching.

The line of thought touching Immortality in the Apocrypha is a true *præparatio evangelica*.

The teaching of our Lord carries the doctrine of the soul to the highest point which it has reached or can reach. It is the supreme insuperable stage in the belief of the soul's Immortality.

But about His teaching in general, and in this matter especially, it needs to be said that He does not so much teach new truths, but He changes the perspective of truths. In His Gospel the soul is not forgotten, nor is the body, but the relation between them is transformed. It is no more the body—no more the present life — that seems important. The body is inconsiderable in comparison of the soul. The present is inconsiderable in comparison of the future.

Our Lord does not teach the present or future existence of the soul. He takes that existence for granted. What he does is to emphasise the intrinsic and absolute moment of the life of the soul. How awful, how impressive are His words! "What is a man profited, if he shall gain the whole world and lose his own soul? or what shall a man give in exchange for his soul?"[1] And again, "Fear not

[1] St. Matthew xvi. 26.

them which kill the body, but are not able to kill the soul; but rather fear Him that is able to destroy both soul and body in hell." [1] That the soul, religiously considered, is of such value as infinitely to transcend all other parts of human nature is, it may be said, an axiom of His creed.

And in conformity to the value which He set, and His disciples after Him, upon the soul was His conception, and theirs in obedience to Him, of His own redeeming work upon the Cross. It was not for the bodies or minds of men that He died, but for their souls. Thus St. Peter says of Him, "Whom having not seen, ye love, in Whom, though now ye see Him not, yet believing ye rejoice with joy unspeakable and full of glory; receiving the end of your faith, even the salvation of your souls." [2]

This is the substance—the very heart—of the Christian Faith.

> "Why all the souls that were were forfeit once,
> And He that might the vantage best have took
> Found out the remedy." [3]

It is the Atonement as taught by the writers of

---

[1] St. Matthew x. 28. [2] 2 Peter i. 8, 9.
[3] Shakespeare, *Measure for Measure*, Act ii. Scene ii.

the New Testament, by St. Paul especially, and by the Fathers of the Church.

Salvation is a spiritual term. It is a deliverance not of the body or the intellect but of the soul, a deliverance not from pains or sorrows or sufferings, but from sin. Nay, it may often happen that physical and mental sufferings are the conditions of spiritual good, and, if so, they are blessings, though in disguise.

The Church of Christ, despite her manifold lapses and errors, has not lost the thought or the sight of her Master's teaching. She may serve the bodily interests of men; she has nobly served them. She has shown by her example that it is not where the body aspires to the first place in the life of Man, but where it holds the second place as inferior to the soul that it attains to its true and proper dignity; asylums, hospitals, infirmaries, and homes of refuge are the witnesses of her charity; but it is not for these things that she exists. She exists to save men's souls. Her Divine Founder was the Healer of men's bodies as well as of their souls, but it was for their souls that He died. And all that the Church has done or can do must be subordinated to her one essential work of saving souls. For this she was born, for this she came into the world; it is her function, her very life, and rather than surrender this she would die. Such is the belief of the Church of Christ, and from it issue two or three consequent beliefs which it is right to specify.

The first is the consciousness of sin. That consciousness is strictly a religious sentiment. Human philosophies ignore or impair the sense of sin. They recognise crime, they do not recognise sin. It is because they have no strong realisation of the soul's personal life. For sin (apart from external consequences) is a stain upon the soul, and, if the soul be that for which the Saviour died, then how terrible is a stain upon it! There is no deeper need of the present day than to revivify the decadent or dying sense of sin.

Yet again, the value set upon the soul in our Lord's teaching affects (as has been already intimated) the estimate of the sorrows, sufferings and disappointments which are inevitable parts of human destiny. It expands the significance of the word "good," which is too often limited to physical and corporeal benefits. But the good of the soul may be the exact opposite of a physical good. A privation which depresses the body may be itself an elevation of the soul. Therefore, the Christian or the religious man in general, having regard to the soul, and not only so but to the soul as endowed with Immortality, may well accept and rejoice in such a fate as is contrary to the dispositions and inclinations of the body. The ascetic life, with its manifold, mysterious applications, depends upon the regard paid to the soul.

It is in the nature of the soul too that there lies the secret of the great distinction which was not known even as a fancy to the classical pagan world, though that world was so clever and refined, but is an axiom of every modern polity—the distinction between the world and the Church, between the secular life and the spiritual, between the things which in their nature are temporal and the things which are eternal and Divine. What the issue of that distinction may be in the coming days none can tell, but it touches the very nature of Man. It determines what should be his character and his conduct in the crises of life. It renders the actions and even the language of one section of society unfamiliar, if not unintelligible, to the other. But if the soul be transcendently greater than the body, then they who render it its due importance will win the day.

The conclusions and inferences of this chapter may be briefly stated as follows :—

The conception, more or less vague, of the human spirit or soul as in its nature surviving the bodily life appears to be universal among the primitive and savage races of mankind. That conception was originally crude and material; it has been slowly refined into spirituality.

It was the destiny of the Jewish people, though they were late in realising the conception of a future spiritual existence, to accept it eventually in its purest form and to commend it most persuasively to mankind.

That conception, first imagined by the Psalmists and prophets, and afterwards purified in the Apocryphal literature, was elevated to its sublime dignity by Jesus Christ. He taught not only the existence and the pure spirituality of the soul, but its paramount superiority to any other part, and to all the other parts, of human nature.

This superiority was the axiom of His own redemptive work. It is equally the axiom of all Christian devotion and philanthropy.

Religion is, in a word, a cultivation of the soul. Beyond this cultivation no religious system or creed can ever rise.

CHAPTER III

VALUE OF THE BELIEF

WE have seen what is the true belief in the soul's Immortality, and how it arose and was historically developed. We have seen that it has been purged, by slow degrees, not without difficulty, of the material grossness originally attaching to it, and has become a pure spiritual faith. But it remains to ask—What is the bearing of this belief upon the common daily practical human life? Would the world be affected, and if so, how affected? would it be the better or the worse, if the belief in Immortality should cease?

This chapter, it is necessary to say, is concerned solely with the value of the belief—not with its truth or its probability, but with its value. There is no assumption that, because a belief is valuable, therefore it is true. It may indeed be urged upon the hypothesis of a beneficent Almighty Providence that it is not probable that Man would be left in the unhappy position of finding a belief to be essential or important to his moral welfare and yet to be false. The belief in God then lends a certain strength to the argument from the value or necessity of any other belief to its truth. But the belief in God may or may not be treated as reasonable. The object of this chapter is to inquire the value of the belief in Immortality without any regard to its validity. But in no part of this essay is candour or moderation more necessary, and in none, perhaps, is it more difficult.

It is argued that men have lived good lives, and even lives of special and remarkable virtue, without the sanction or motive of an immortal hope; that they have loved righteousness for its own sake, without any thought of reward or penalty; and that it is a foolish policy therefore to make the duty or possibility of virtuous living dependent in any sense upon a belief which has been shown to be not essential, and which may not improbably prove to be fallacious. It is better, according to this argument, so to educate and discipline mankind, that they may feel virtue to be its own reward.

That good and noble lives have been lived in the

absence of religious belief, in the absence of a belief in Immortality, is probable enough; it will readily be admitted by Christians. There is not so much virtue in the world that it can be right or wise to disparage what there is. The theory that human nature is absolutely corrupt is disproved by human nature itself. And if it were absolutely corrupt, it would be incapable of responding to the appeal which religion makes to it, and religion would languish or die. The sanctions and motives of religion do not re-create human nature; they take it as it is; they elevate and purify it; they could not find root in human nature if the soil were utterly hard. No doubt the virtue as well as the vice of human nature may be exaggerated. Anti-Christian writers have made too much of the one, as Christian writers of the other; for human nature is not wholly good or wholly bad, but is composed of good and bad qualities in differing degrees, although, if no external influences were brought to bear upon it, it would probably sink, instead of rising, in moral dignity. But Theology forfeits the confidence of sensible and reasonable thinkers, if it denies such tendencies to goodness as exist in human nature, for the sake of magnifying the work of the Divine grace in human hearts and lives. That human nature is crossed, as it were, by a dark streak or flaw, which is what is called in the language of Theology "original sin," is one belief; that it is absolutely vile is quite another. The former accords with the facts of conscience and history. The latter is a desperate conclusion to which men have not come spontaneously, but have felt themselves driven at times by the cogency of their own theological premisses. Still, grave as is the mistake of representing human nature bad, it is a yet graver mistake to represent it as wholly good. The simple truth of human nature seems to be that it is prone partly to goodness, partly to evil; but that, if it is to ascend to a high moral elevation, it needs all, or more than all, the help and support that systems of belief or laws of conduct have ever afforded it.

Upon a study of human history or of the human soul it is impossible to doubt that Man, in spite of his innate promptings to righteousness, can ill-afford to dispense with any incentive or motive to virtuous living. But of such incentives the belief in God, and, as its corollary, the belief in Immortality, is the strongest. And it is only too sadly apparent that human nature, though it be reinforced with this strong motive to morality, has found hard work in making its way through failure and suffering to the gates of the Celestial City.

It is not indeed altogether safe to argue from the assumed integrity of certain lives, whether Christian or non-Christian. Men are not in general competent judges of each other's lives. They see only what is obvious and external. It is God who reads the heart. His alone is the unerring Judgment-Seat. Of the sacred rules laid down by Christ for human conduct none is more equitable or charitable than this, "Judge not, that ye be not judged." The fallibility of human, the accuracy of Divine judgment, are the principles which nerve and inspire the personal life. It is right that man should be judged, but that he should be judged by One Whose judgment is just. For except upon the supposition of a Divine Almighty Judgment, it seems that there is no security, and little probability, that justice will be done to individuals in this life or afterwards.

It may be admitted, however, that men have lived good lives without the sanction of religion. It may be admitted too, that men possessing religious faith have often failed in the practice of virtue. But to make these admissions is not to admit that religious faith as a motive is ineffectual. It is only to allow—what experience attests—that motives are not so influential as they ought in logic to be upon human lives. Man is not a creature of reason only, but of desire, emotion, sentiment, as well as reason ; and the fact that motives do not always work their logical effect, is an argument, not for destroying or impairing, but for fortifying the motives. For motives are operative in proportion to their own strength and to the strength of the belief with which men apprehend them ; if they are inadequate therefore, it is necessary to strengthen them.

And when it is said that virtue is its own reward, this is a statement which may be either a truism or a paradox. To whom is virtue its own reward ? Not indeed to everybody ; so much is plain ; for if virtue were everywhere its own reward, and were known to be so, the world would be virtuous ; it would not be, as in fact it is, a scene of tangled good and evil, where generous aspirations are too often marred by deep and melancholy failures. Man, it has been said, stands alone among animate beings, in that he recognises and admits his own true interest and yet acts against it. Such human action is indisputable ; but it is an evidence that virtue, if it is sometimes a pleasure, is or may be at other times a painful sacrifice. Suppose that a person who has lived long years in sin determines to break by resolute effort the bands of sinful habit, as when a drunkard takes the pledge of abstinence from drink; his virtuous action is not pleasant to him, but painful; it is so painful that he often sinks under the burden of it. The first step in the path of penitence must be difficult; there are times when it cannot be taken except under the constraining influence of a belief in the righteous anger of God against iniquity.

It is true indeed that one, who begins by abstaining from evil in the belief that it will involve shame or punishment, may in the end rise to so high a moral elevation as to find in the practice of virtue not only a pleasure but a passionate delight. This, however, is the supreme attainment of the moral life. Few are they—and those the saints—who have aspired to it. What a wilful error it would be to treat a temper so sublime as if it were the common lot of ordinary men and women! The love of virtue for its own sake is the reward of those who have practised virtue as a hard duty. It is not the sinner who loves virtue, but the saint. Yet saints are few, and sinners many, and how a sinner may be brought to lead the saintly life is the most difficult problem of religion or morality.

The law of the moral life, has nowhere, I think, been expressed more truly than in a passage of the ancient Greek poet, Hesiod, "Thou mayest choose vice and plenty of it, and the choice shall not be hard. The path is smooth, and vice dwells at thy door. But the immortal Gods have set toil at the threshold of virtue; long and arduous is the way thereto, and at the first it is rough; but when a man has reached the summit, then is virtue easy, though so hard." [1] It is the privilege of the saint not only to practise virtue but to love it. To one who has spent his life in sanctity, virtue may be, and often is, its own reward. It is so to him, it is not so to others. The sinner, to whom his sin is not a pain, but, at least for a time, a satisfaction, needs an overmastering motive, if he is to turn his back upon sin and to set his face towards the vision of holiness. The faith in Immor-

---

[1] Hesiod, *Works and Days*, 285 sqq.:

> τὴν μέν τοι κακότητα καὶ ἰλαδὸν ἔστιν ἐλέσθαι
> ῥηϊδίως· λείη μὲν ὁδός, μάλα δ' ἐγγύθι νάιει.
> τῆς δ'ἀρετῆς ἱδρῶτα θεοὶ προπάροιθεν ἔθηκαν
> ἀθάνατοι· μακρὸς δὲ καὶ ὄρθιος οἶμος ἐς αὐτὴν
> καὶ τρηχὺς τοπρῶτον· ἐπὴν δ'εἰς ἄκρον ἵκηται,
> ῥηϊδίη δὴ ἔπειτα πέλει, χαλεπή περ ἐοῦσα.

tality affords this motive, and there is no other faith that equally affords it. It is impossible to deny or dispute the bearing of the faith in Immortality upon conduct, unless it be supposed either that human nature stands in no need of motives to virtue, or that motives do not influence action. But these suppositions are untenable. They display a singular ignorance of the human nature to which they relate; they render the theory of conduct not logical or intelligible but chaotic. For Man has sore need, as experience proves, of the incentives and inducements to virtue.

How can it be argued that men are enamoured of virtue and disposed to practise it with a pure, unselfish affection, when the world is strewn with the wreckage of lives, and hopes are frustrate and opportunities wasted and promises end in despair? How can it be said in the face of fraud and cruelty and lust? How can it be said by any one who studies himself or the world? The history of humanity and the conscience of each man are alike the witnesses that the waves of interest and passion are ceaselessly surging against the barrier of human morality and threatening to sweep it away.

Historically Man has been a bad judge of human

nature. The theologians of old, as has been said, could discern in it nothing but evil. Some modern thinkers have seemed to discern nothing but good. Yet it is simply absurd to speak as though men were everywhere and always inclined to righteousness, if only they could find some sufficient reason for following it. The theological doctrine of innate sinfulness is probably truer than the opposite doctrine of innate righteousness. He who knows himself knows that good and evil are ever at war within his soul, and that, if he is to refuse the evil and to choose the good, he needs the strongest possible motive to morality. For to him the Apostle's words are vividly present as expressing the truth of his own personal experience. "I find then a law, that, when I would do good, evil is present with me. For I delight in the law of God after the inward man; but I see another law in my members, warring against the law of my mind, and bringing me into captivity to the law of sin which is in my members. O wretched man that I am! Who shall deliver me from the body of this death?"[1]

So evident is the testimony of human nature to

[1] Romans vii. 21-24.

sin as a fact and to the consequent need of moral sanctions. Nor is the connexion of belief with conduct less evident. For if action, *i.e.*, rational action, is not caused by belief, how is it caused? On what principle does a man choose one line of action rather than another? The reason lies, as is plain, in his belief. He believes the line which he chooses to be right or necessary or expedient. He believes that he will be rewarded for taking it or punished if he does not take it, whatever the form of reward or punishment may be, and thus his choice is made.

Actions then, so far as they are reasonable, are the consequences of belief. It is belief which determines the choice of actions.

No doubt the choice is not always, as it ought to be, consistently made. Beliefs do not always dominate action; for it is subject to counterbalancing influences such as desires, sentiments, interests, and the like. Beliefs, too, may be more or less cogent; one belief is authoritative, another persuasive, another so faint as to be only suggestive. But it remains true that, so far as action is reasonable, it depends on belief; there is nothing else on which it can depend. And if it be so, then there is no belief which is naturally qualified to exercise such influence upon conduct as the faith in Immortality. For when full allowance has been made, as it ought to be made, for the circumstances by which the natural effect of belief upon action is more or less modified, it is mere playing with facts to argue that one, who limits his view of responsibility to the present life and to such laws and sanctions as are operative in it, possesses the same imperious motive to a moral life as one who holds that for all the actions and intentions of his life he is ultimately responsible after death at the bar of an Almighty and Omniscient Judge. The believer in a retributory Immortality is far more strongly bound to virtue than others who lack this or any such belief; and if the moral level of his life is not higher than theirs, his culpability is proportionately greater.

The moral value then of a belief in Immortality may now be taken as established. But although the faith in Immortality, with such convictions as issue from it, may be the most potent motive to morality, it is not the only motive. Writers both ancient and modern have sometimes set its value too high. Thus Cicero says—but who will justify his words?

—"Nemo unquam sine magna spe immortalitatis se pro patria offerret ad mortem."[1] Similarly the great French preacher Massillon, in his discourse on the Immortality of the Soul, says, "La société universelle des hommes, les lois qui nous unissent les uns aux autres, les devoirs les plus sacrés et les plus inviolables de la vie civile, tout cela n'est fondé que sur la certitude d'un avenir. Ainsi si tout meurt avec le corps, il faut que l'univers prenne d'autres lois, d'autres mœurs, d'autres usages, et que tout change de face sur la terre. Les maximes de l'équité, de l'amitié, de l'honneur, de la bonne foi, de la reconnaissance ne sont plus que des erreurs populaires, puisque nous ne devons rien à des hommes, qui ne nous sont rien, auxquels aucun nœud commun de culte et d'espérance ne nous lie, qui vont demain retomber dans le néant, et qui ne sont déjà plus."[2] But the supreme value of a faith in Immortality has been nowhere put in stronger language than by Robert Hall in his once famous sermon on *Modern Infidelity considered with respect to its Influence on Society*. The

---

[1] "No one would ever expose himself to death for his country if he had not a strong hope of Immortality."—*Tusc. Disp.*, i. 15, 32.
[2] *De l'Immortalité de l'Âme.*

following passage will serve as a specimen of his argument :—

"As the present world, on sceptical principles, is the only place of recompense, whenever the practice of virtue fails to promise the greatest sum of present good (cases which often occur in reality and much oftener in appearance) every motive to virtuous conduct is superseded; a deviation from rectitude becomes the part of wisdom, and should the path of virtue, in addition to this, be obstructed by disgrace, torment or death, to persevere would be madness or folly, and a violation of the first and most essential law of Nature. Virtue, on these principles, being in numberless instances at war with self-preservation, never can or ought to become a fixed habit of the mind."

Such passages are no doubt guilty of exaggeration. For the truth is that under all moral systems, whether actual or possible, some men will be virtuous and others vicious, and still more, men will, in their characters, exhibit varied blendings or interlacings of virtue and vice. Nor indeed is the habit of mind which takes pleasure in classifying men as good or evil, saved or unsaved, Christian or non-Christian, in any high degree salutary or charitable. Divine Omniscience alone can distinguish the tares from the wheat in the harvest-field of life; to the Divine Master men alike stand or fall. It is wise to discuss the natural tendencies rather than the actual results of moral systems; for it is a safe assumption that soon or late the natural tendencies will develope and display themselves in experience.

The singular advantage of the belief in Immortality is that it provides a sanction, and other beliefs do not, for the exceptional or extreme cases of moral duty. For a moral system must be tested by extreme cases. It must provide an adequate sanction for morality not only in the ordinary, but in the special and sublime, decisions of life. If such a system does not meet the extreme cases, if it does not in these cases satisfy the demand of the conscience, then it will ultimately fail in other cases.

It is rightly demanded then that a moral system should justify the supreme manifestations of human virtue. If it is incapable of producing saints and martyrs, or, in other words, of justifying sanctity and martyrdom, it will soon or late fail to produce men and women, or to produce many men and women, of the virtue which is now assumed to be general among Christians. For a moral system tends ultimately to produce such consequences as ordinary people deduce from its principles. No moral system of antiquity was illumined by a brighter example in its founder's life than Epicureanism; but the name of Epicurus has in history become no more than a synonym for a *bon vivant;* and it has become so because Epicurus preached the doctrine of pleasure, and men have accepted from him his special doctrine, and have interpreted it according to their own disposition.

It may be taken for granted then that a moral system, whatever it may be, will not in practice ultimately rise to a higher level than the interpretation which ordinary men and women put upon its principles. And here perhaps Robert Hall's sermon may be quoted once more, " By great and sublime virtues are meant those which are called into action on great and trying occasions, which demand the sacrifice of the dearest interests and prospects of human life and sometimes of life itself ; the virtues, in a word, which by their rarity and splendour draw admiration, and have rendered illustrious the character of patriots, martyrs, and confessors. It requires but little reflexion to perceive that whatever veils a future world and contracts the limits of existence within the present life must tend in a proportionable degree to diminish the grandeur and narrow the sphere of human agency."

The matter then would appear to stand in this way. The belief in Immortality supplies a sanction for all virtues. There is no discipline—no sacrifice—so great that it cannot be justified upon the plain assumption that God Who is Almighty will at His pleasure within the eternal spaces of futurity recompense and satisfy all such virtuous actions as are performed, at whatever present loss or sorrow, for His sake.

It is here that upon a secular system of morality the ultimate coincidence of virtue with happiness, which is the postulate of the human conscience, seems to fail.

The difficulty of such a system is to provide a moral sanction for the noblest actions. For such a system this life is all. Morality is relative to this life. It must find its sanction, its justification in this life. Life becomes then, if not the *summum bonum*, yet the condition under which alone the *summum bonum* is attainable. Secular morality, as it follows, cannot justify to the individual the sacrifice of his life for any cause. To say so is not to say that men have not sacrificed their lives for truth and honour without the faith in a personal Immortality. Men are not seldom better than their creeds. But it is to say that the sacrifice of life is not justifiable upon secular principles. The martyr acts nobly but irrationally, as there is no recompense possible to him when life is taken from him. That "he who loses his life shall find it" is not a belief which secular morality can entertain. The world has instinctively felt the danger which belongs to the loss of faith in the soul's Immortality. It shrinks from the thought of an atheistical society.

Yet if it is asked what would be the necessary consequence of a purely secular morality, it is perhaps not so much that the world would immediately lose virtuous conduct as that it would lose the fine or delicate flower of virtue. It would lose in fact not virtue but sanctity. Sanctity is the flower or fragrance of virtue. How shall I speak of it? It is to virtue what grace is to behaviour, what expression is to beauty. It elevates by spiritualising, as grace by refining. It is something added to virtue, something higher than virtue. The saint does often the same actions as the moral person, only he does them in a different way. He is free from worldliness. He thinks not of himself. He breathes a serener atmosphere than other men. He is nearer to God.

The difference between sanctity and mere dutifulness was seen, it is said, in the hospitals of Paris, when the Sisters of Mercy yielded their place to secular nurses. The duty done was the same, yet not the same; it missed the special charm of devotion, of piety. What, then, was the secret of this charm? It is told that the Sisters whose task is hardest and most painful, such as they who spend their lives in ministering to the fallen abandoned women in the great cities, sometimes feel their hearts sinking within them at the contact with so great and terrible impurity; then they retire into the little chapel set apart for them and pray awhile before the altar, and when their prayer is finished, they are strengthened again for their ministry.

It was even so with the Master Himself, Who "continued all night in prayer to God."

This, or such as this, is indeed the flower of sanctity. It is not the avoidance only, but the abhorrence of evil. It is not the practice only, but the joy of devotion. Yet it is in the power of loving souls, however weak. It is delicacy, refinement, purity, yet sacrifice too. In it is something that is unearthly, something Divine. For it issues chiefly or solely from the example of Him Who, being in the world, was yet not of it, but lived above it in the perfectness of an immaculate purity; for Him alone among the children of men evil could not approach or defile, and from the cradle to the Cross there rested not upon His soul even the passing shadow of sin.

This it is that the world will lose, if it loses religion.

Yet is there no greater sorrow than the loss of an ideal. For though the ideal be never realised, it has the power of attracting thoughts and hopes and desires upwards to itself.

Sanctity is rare among men. The saints are few; but the world is saved by its saints. They alone, it may be, ascend to the highest height, and their feet are set on the untrodden snow; but others struggling heavenwards from the lowlands take hope from the vision of the saints. The beliefs and habits of religion constitute the saintly life. Apart from them there would in the end be no saints. And it may be feared that, when the supreme attainment of virtue is done away, the moral standard of the world would gradually be lowered.

And not only would the moral standard be lowered, but morality itself would suffer a change. Morality is a word of various meaning; it did not mean the same thing in the ancient classical as in the modern world; it would not mean the same thing in an infidel as in a religious society. For the virtues which relate to or depend on Immortality, such as the reverence for human life, the habit of worship, the culture of purity, would languish, if Immortality were no longer a faith. Every religion has its own morality, and the morality approved, if not always practised, in Christian society, is the morality which Jesus Christ taught.

Thus the value of the belief in Immortality is a conclusion arising from a just estimate of human nature.

While it is admitted that the virtuous tendencies of Humanity are the ground upon which the hope of human progress rests, it remains true that the moral dignity of man is less positive and stable than it is sometimes imagined to be. Human virtue cannot yet make boast of itself. It is not an immutable fact. The best of men are not far removed from the worst sins. Humanity stands, as it were, on the slope of a high mountain, it breathes the pure and bracing air of Heaven, but it may soon and easily lose its footing and sink backwards into the depths which lie below.

Great and awful, then, is the responsibility of those who would cut away any sanction or support of the moral life. But the chief of these sanctions and supports is Immortality.

The faith in Immortality, then, if it be lost, is irreplaceable.

But it is not only the morality of individuals which is at stake in the battle of belief; it is also the morality, and with it the felicity, of nations.

And here it is perhaps worth while to notice that it is not so much the wealthy or privileged or cultivated classes who are so dependent upon a faith in Immortality; it is, however little they may themselves know it, the poor, the ignorant, the unhappy, the debased. The faith of these classes may be tacit or inarticulate or concealed, as their faith in God is often; but if it exists, though lying ever so deep within them, it is a check upon wild action and a solace in the sufferings of life. It cannot, I think, be proved, but neither can it be denied, that the social and political movements, indicating in many European countries a discontent and an impatience which are dangerous signs of the time, are largely the outcome of the speculations which have taught men, in the name of Philosophy or Science or any other name, to cast away the restraining power of belief in God. Certainly it is remarkable that that discontent or impatience in its most pronounced form, when it calls itself anarchism, is equally intolerant and contemptuous of authority, human and Divine; it treats the laws of men with as little respect as the laws of God. And, indeed, if the faith of the people in God and Immortality is done away, and their privations, their labours, their sufferings remain, is it reasonable to think that they will acquiesce in an inequality which was always hard to bear and is now felt to be hopeless, because it fills the whole space of their existence?

The faith in Immortality where it exists is always a motive—the strongest of all motives—to a patient self-restraint. And not only so, but that faith, whether among individuals or among nations, is a spur to moral action. He who possesses it, however often he may have failed, yet possesses in himself the potency of better things. For human life, if it be complete within itself, does not authorise an absolute morality. It is the doctrine of Immortality which harmonises duty and reward. For Immortality throws its protecting shield over the whole wide field of human duty. It is the promise that no resolute effort or generous service, no refusal of sin, no persistency in virtue, no cup of cold water given in charity to a disciple shall lose its reward. Within the sphere of Immortality lies the justification for all the demands that conscience makes of Humanity.

But it is not only as a moral motive, it is also as a moral satisfaction, that the belief in Immortality commends itself to human hearts. It is the one belief that sets and can set the mind at rest in the contemplation of the ways of Providence.

It is well to consider what is the proper attitude of the finite human mind towards an Infinite Intelligence. *Ex hypothesi* such a mind is impotent to understand the full scope of the Providential scheme. It must confess the limitations and imperfections of its knowledge. That there should be difficulties in the human estimate of Providence is only a way of saying that Providence is Divine. But it were wrong to look upon these difficulties as only so many intellectual hardships; they are moral tests; and it is as tests that they are essential elements in the Divine dealings with mankind.

It is necessary, then, that Man, as a finite being, should be subject to doubt in his apprehension of Divine Providence. Mystery is the element in which Man lives as Man. But mystery, however natural, is none the less painful; if it be hopeless, it may become intolerable.

What is it, then, that Man may reverently and not unreasonably ask of God? It is that the mystery of life, if as yet unsolved, should not be proved to be insoluble. He may not demand to see the solution in this life, but he cannot forego the hope that it will be seen hereafter. Faith, in short, will carry him as far as, but no further than, the words: "What I do thou knowest not now, but thou shalt know hereafter." That his present knowledge is imperfect he may admit; that it can never be completed he will deny.

Thus the relation of man to God is, in familiar language, as that of a child to his earthly father whose motives he cannot understand but whose goodness he trusts implicitly. He waits, but his waiting is full of hope. He reposes his trust in God. The curtain hangs, as it were, between him and the truth on which his heart is set; he cannot tell, he can scarcely imagine, what is hidden behind it, but he knows that some day the curtain will be lifted. Thus the discipline of this life, the anticipation of a life after this, are the consequences issuing from the fact of an Invisible Immortal Will in which he believes.

This hope or this faith naturally influences the Christian view of life taken as a whole. Life is not free from puzzling and distressing features. The inequalities of life, for instance, cannot but excite a certain feeling of sadness in the mind. It is a just moral expectation that all men should ultimately enjoy a fair or equal chance of happiness, whether it be given them in the present or in the future. But upon a survey of the present life men are not equal; they do not enjoy the same or nearly the same chances. The disparity which exists between them is not merely or principally relative to such goods as are called external, *e.g.*, wealth or social circumstances or honour, and if it were so, it would be easily overrated; for of these goods the influence upon happiness is probably less than it seems to be, as the enjoyment depends upon the sense of need, when they are wanting, or of appreciation, when they are attained. There is reason to think that, if it were possible to compare the tastes, desires and satisfactions of two persons taken from opposite or widely different social strata, the positive inequality of happiness would often be found to be slight. Still differences of place and privilege exist, and they affect the character or condition of life. One man is born in such circumstances as facilitate the cultivation of virtuous habits, another is the victim of hereditary taint or vicious example or base associations. Or again, the sin of one man is visited with a life-long stigma ; another, who may be a worse sinner, goes unpunished. No view of the present human life taken in itself can adequately interpret these inequalities ; they postulate the justice of the Almighty acting in an Immortal Existence. Thus the belief in Immortality is in effect the belief that an equalisation of human destinies (subject, of course, to human freedom) will be realised at the last.

Pain again is a mystery which has always weighed upon the sensitive conscience of mankind. If it be considered in relation to the present life, and to that alone, it must be said to lack not only beneficence, but in a great degree significance. For pain is not intelligible, as an element in experience, unless it be educative. It must promise, it must more or less promote, a future blessing. In this life its educative effect is not always seen. But assume an Immortal Life, and pain becomes at once a discipline of whose beneficence Man is permitted to catch a glimpse even in this life. For pain contains in itself a moralising or sanctifying power. Human nature, being constituted as it is, can afford as little to dispense with pain as it can with death. Death is the great solemnising power; it redeems life from flippancy, it constrains the most thoughtless souls to pause and think. Pain too is the spring of generous sympathies and sacrifices. Nay, not so only; but it is the special function of pain to evoke the sentiments and qualities which are preparatory, as it were, to the Eternal Life. Humility, patience, resignation, faith, devotion are spiritual qualities, and, as such, they are prophetic of Immortality. It follows that pain, although in human eyes it may seem mere loss or indignity, is in the Divine view a scarcely veiled benediction. Pain is a mark of Divine favour, as it creates the temper or character which is pleasing to God. Thus it is true that "whom the Lord loveth He chasteneth and scourgeth every son whom He receiveth."[1]

[1] Hebrews xii. 6.

Lastly, death, though it ceases not to be terrible, is in the view of Immortality not intolerable. It were a hopeless evil, if it were the end. It is not, or not necessarily, an evil, if it be not the end of life, but a stage or an incident in life itself, if it is, as an ancient writer says, "midway in life."[1] But this is the religious view; it is the Christian view. It leaves the future dark yet vast; it does not shut the door on hope. It invests with deep and awful, yet blessed, possibility the shadowy spaces which lie behind the veil.

There is no beatitude vouchsafed to man so great as this. No discovery of Philosophy or Art or Science is so rich in its solace for anguished souls as the revelation of Immortality. That One greater than death holds the keys of hell and death is the supreme belief to which Humanity rises. I dare to say that without it life is not worth living. But to those who embrace it life is hopeful, it is sacred, it is Divine.

In the faith of Immortality, then, lies the solution of the mystery encircling life and death. What the

---

[1] Lucan, *Pharsalia* 1,457 (of the Druids).
"Longæ canitis si cognita vitæ
Mors media est."

ultimate solution may be Man knows not. But he knows that it is there. In that knowledge he is content—nay, happy. His life rests upon God.

So it is that the doctrine of Immortality not only coheres, as has been said, with the faith in God, but is indispensable to it. The eternity of God and the eternity of the individual life are the keys to the interpretation of Providence.

The doctrine of Immortality is of infinite value, alike as affording an absolute sanction for the efforts and sacrifices of virtue, and as yielding strength to human nature in its anxieties, and solace in its bitter bereavements. So far, however, it has been treated only in its relation to the Divine Economy. It has been shown to be a necessary condition of the belief in a Providential Government of the world.

But every doctrine which expresses, or seeks to express, the relation of Man to God has its human side as well as its Divine. It will necessarily answer to the demand of human nature in itself, *i.e.*, without regard to the view which man may take of Providence.

Thus it is necessary in considering Immortality to consider some special features of Man's nature.

For the object of this chapter is to inquire what would be the loss of virtue or happiness, if men were forbidden to speculate religiously upon the future. This loss will be the measure of the value which properly belongs to the belief.

The passionate longing of mankind for a deathless life may be regarded, and will hereafter be regarded, as an argument. It is here to be treated as a need. It is a need which Immortality satisfies, and no other doctrine or theory can satisfy it.

The desire of man for Immortality has not always and everywhere been equally strong. In some, if not all, of the more refined and cultivated races of mankind it has been and is so powerful as to amount to an irresistible prejudice. And upon the whole, the greater the refinement or the cultivation of the race, the more intense is the longing for Immortality.

This desire is in general independent of special conditions attaching to the Immortal Life. It is not a desire for equalisation or retribution or advancement. It is a desire for existence. It is an intuitive consciousness of persistency. In Mr. Alger's words, " It seems clear that the real belief in Immortality did not originate from the contemplation of the phenomena of dreams and shadows and echoes, but arose from the inexpugnable self-assertion of consciousness, its inability to feel itself non-existent." [1]

This desire, however interpreted, is the more remarkable, as it seems to distinguish Man broadly from the other animals to which his physical structure and character are akin. It is right to speak of those animals with reserve; so little is known of their nature or sentiments; but at least the appearance is that they take death, like life itself, as a natural thing, without any wonder or difficulty or pain. Man alone resents and regrets the idea of death. He refuses to die. He would sooner live in pain than perish in peace. He demands for himself unending life. Of all strange and striking facts in human history none throws more light upon man's inalienable desire of Immortality, than that an everlasting doom of woe should have been found in the history of thought a creed less intolerable than annihilation or absolute death.

But there is another way in which it is possible to form some estimate of the loss which would fall upon Humanity, if by any arbitrary or self-imposed

[1] *A Critical History of the Doctrine of a Future Life*, p. 728.

decree it were forbidden to mankind to extend the range of their thoughts and hopes and even their beliefs beyond and above the limits of the present life ; and what can be said of it but that it would be a blight covering the face of all the earth ? It would be a narrowing or impoverishing of all that makes human nature sublime. The spring of imagination and devotion would be dried up. In whatever direction the human spirit might seek to move, it would be stayed as if by some invisible bar.

Literature is a witness that human life or thought, if it were cut off from the hope of Immortality, would become a sterilised thing. For the masterpieces of literary genius, whether ancient or modern, are largely occupied with questions relating to the invisible world. If Man were limited to the present, if he might not in fancy or belief speculate upon the destiny of the soul when it passes at death beyond the sphere of sense, what would become—it is not necessary to say of the sacred books of all religions—but of the *Odyssey* or the *Prometheus Vinctus* or the *Alcestis* or the *Æneid* or the *Divina Commedia* or *Hamlet* or *Paradise Lost* or *In Memoriam* ? The invisible world and all that belongs to it have been the nursery of great thoughts and burning aspirations. To the high theme of Immortality poets, artists, and philosophers, no less than preachers or theologians, have been drawn by an irresistible attraction. They have spent upon it reverent, earnest thought and labour. How much light has been so shed upon the darkness encompassing the future of the soul is not now the question. It is enough that in seeking to illumine the darkness (even though the effort has been made in vain), they have enlarged and enriched the spiritual thoughts of Humanity, and have lifted them to a brighter and purer world.

For, apart from all particular theories of Immortality, it is the belief in a personal Immortal Life of human souls which gives Man his proper dignity in the scale of Nature. As Science lowers him in his own eyes, Theology exalts him. On the one hand he is little higher than the beasts; on the other hand he is little lower than the angels. For Our Lord in the mysterious passage in which He speaks of the angels, says explicitly that they "die not." Death is the lot of Humanity. Deathlessness is the boon of the angelic life. Spiritual beings, as the angels, cannot die. So too the spirit of Man, as being itself immortal, approximates to the angelic life.

There is much in Nature which tends to overpower human thought. The vast spaces of Astronomy, the vast periods of Geology, stand in contrast with the narrow limits of human being. The mighty powers which Nature now and again puts forth in the earthquake or the hurricane or the cataclysm reduce Man's physical activity to insignificance. What is to be set against this great overmastering thought? It can be nothing else than the belief that Man possesses in himself an immortal treasure, and that treasure is the soul. The soul is the witness of its own eternity as of its own spirituality. It is, as Democritus said, "the house of God."[1] Or as Epictetus said, every man "carries about a God within him." To know this truth is to know the dignity of Man.

It is no part of this essay to discuss the theory of Man's origin. But among the seeming evidences of a lost potency or capacity, as of a vision half-forgotten yet half-remembered, is his dissatisfaction with himself and the conditions of his being. He does not think of himself as of one whose history

[1] ψυχὴ οἰκητήριον δαίμονος.

had been a continuous progress from a lower to a higher state. He has felt always that he might be better than he is, and ought to do more than he has ever done. He is conscious of powers which do not find full play in this world. He is oppressed by the sense of contrast between his ideal and the realisation which falls so far short of it. Hence his spirit is for ever in unrest. What a pain there is in human inability to do more work ! How wasteful and saddening seem the hours spent in sleep ! The limitations of his physical senses are distressful to him. The imperfection of his moral nature jars upon his conscience. He feels within himself the yearnings for a sanctity not of earth. Nay, as he looks around him his pathetic regret is only intensified. He erects buildings, and they outlive him. He makes calculations, such as Halley's, and he may not live to verify them. His purposes are immortal. His earthly life closes as a tale that is told. With infinite hopes and aspirations, with poor sinful deeds, striving and failing and learning by failure to strive again, he seems to himself as a prince immured in a gloomy prison house.

But let Man, so cramped and saddened, be suddenly invested with the promise or potency of an everlasting life; then his being assumes a new dignity, as being fraught with endless issues; his actions, his very thoughts bear the stamp of Immortality; he is as a pauper who has succeeded unexpectedly to an inheritance of vast and ample riches. "I am fully persuaded that one of the best springs of generous and worthy actions, is the having generous and worthy thoughts of ourselves. Whoever has a mean opinion of the dignity of his nature, will act in no higher a rank than he has allotted himself in his own estimation. If he considers his being as circumscribed by the uncertain term of a few years, his designs will be contracted into the same narrow span he imagines is to bound his existence. How can he exalt his thoughts to anything great and noble who only believes that after a short term on the stage of this world, he is to sink into oblivion and to lose his consciousness for ever?"[1]

Thus it is true that the belief in Immortality dignifies life as nothing else can dignify it.

> "Life is real! Life is earnest!
> And the grave is not its goal.
> 'Dust thou art, to dust returnest,'
> Was not spoken of the soul."[2]

---

[1] *Spectator*, No. 210.   [2] Longfellow, *A Psalm of Life*.

The assurance of Immortality is generally proportionate to the elevation of the personal life. As Dr. Martineau has said : "The great essential to this belief is a sufficiently elevated estimate of human nature ; no man will ever deny its Immortality who has a deep impression of its capacity for so great a destiny." [1]

But conversely the belief in Immortality inspires great thoughts of the potency lying in the present life. He who is possessed with the thought of his own immortal being, and of that being especially as spiritual, will make it his aim, in the noble words of a pagan philosopher, "to live as far as possible an immortal life." [2]

What then is the character of that life ? This is a question which will be more fully considered hereafter. The Immortal Life must depend, as has been seen, upon the constitution of human nature. All the parts of human nature possess their own graces. But the graces of the body, though beautiful and splendid, are evidently transient. Long before the approach of death they are seen to decay. The soul, too, has its graces, partly intellectual, partly

---

[1] *Five Points of Christian Faith*, p. 19.
[2] ἐφ' ὅσον ἐνδέχεται ἀθανατίζειν, Aristotle, *Nicom. Eth.* x. 7, 8.

emotional; and they too, the intellectual especially, tend to decay. For if the affection remains strong and vivid to life's end, as often it will, yet memory, perception and resolution begin to fail. The spiritual experiences, on the other hand, grow more intense as life proceeds. The consciousness of God is never so clear as at life's close.

Thus the contemplation of the Immortal Life evokes the qualities which seem to possess in themselves the secret of Immortality. He who hopes to live after death will even in this life practise the virtuous habits which do not seem to die.

The habit or temper of *worship*, for instance, is suited to Immortality. Worship is Man's prerogative. It exalts him above other terrestrial beings by prostrating him before the throne of the Supreme. No misjudgment of human nature can be so grievous as the imagination that it is exalted, if it loses the power of looking upwards. Man is never so low as when he thinks great thoughts of himself; he is never so high as when upon his knees he cries, "I have sinned." But humiliation, penitence, devotion, are essentially witnesses to the Unseen. In worship Man asserts his proper kinship with the superior beings whose immaculate existence finds its consummation in worship. It is thus that in the highest aspirations given to Man we adore the Supreme saying, "With Angels and Archangels and all the company of heaven we laud and magnify Thy glorious Name; evermore praising Thee and saying, Holy, holy, holy, Lord God of hosts, Heaven and earth are full of thy glory; glory be to thee, O Lord Most High."

Yet, again, the quality of *love* transcends the grave. St. Paul in a memorable passage has defined it. Yet it is often misunderstood, or but partly understood. Love which asks for love in return is but half love. Love in its nature is selfless; it gives all, it asks for nothing. It is the most ethereal of the virtues. It is greater than faith, greater than hope. It is begun on earth; it is perfected in Heaven. It cannot die. It forbids the thought of mortality. It is immortal as God is immortal. For it is His Spirit; it is Himself; for "God is love."

And akin to love, as a sign and earnest of the Immortal Life, is *purity*. But of this so much only may here be said, that to the believer in Immortality, *i.e.*, to one who believes in the spiritual and eternal nature of Man, it possesses a value which no mere secular system of morals can impart to it; for it is felt to be essentially an approximation of human nature to the Immortal and Divine.

This is the religious faith in its highest form, not Christian faith only; for the most spiritually minded of pagan philosophers puts it thus : " It may well be that none but the pure may approach the pure." [1] And in so saying he does but anticipate the teaching given long ages afterwards by the most spiritual of Christian Apostles. " We know that when He shall appear we shall be like Him; for we shall see Him as He is. And every man that hath this hope in him purifieth himself, even as He is pure." [2]

This chapter has been persuasive and suggestive rather than didactic ; it has in a measure dealt with experiences unknown or hardly known unless, perhaps, to devout and spiritual natures; but its conclusions may be summarised as follows :—

That the belief in Immortality, as interpreted by the enlightened conscience of Humanity, affords, and alone affords, an absolute moral sanction for all the critical sublime demands and duties of life.

That it alone affords a complete infallible solace for all human sufferings, trials and disappointments.

---

[1] Plato, *Phædo*, p. 67, B. μὴ καθαρῷ γὰρ καθαροῦ ἐφάπτεσθαι μὴ οὐ θεμιτὸν ᾖ.   [2] 1 John iii. 2, 3.

That it promises a development and satisfaction of the graces, powers, and capacities which are felt to be circumscribed and sometimes defeated in the present life.

That it exalts and ennobles the whole conception of human nature.

That it guarantees the supreme virtues of Humanity, such as devotion, love, and purity, which are the points of contact between the Divine and human natures.

And that, as so doing, it attests that Man is made in the image of God, and can shape himself according to his Divine Original.

In Pascal's words, then, "Il importe à toute la vie de savoir si l'âme est mortelle ou immortelle."[1]

[1] *Pensées*, ii. 18.

CHAPTER IV

EVIDENCES FOR THE BELIEF

A. *External Evidences*

WHEN the nature of the belief in the soul's Immortality and the development and value of the belief have been ascertained, it is right to examine such evidences as are adducible either for or against the belief itself. For the naturalness or the utility or comfort of a belief is not in itself a proof that the belief is true. A belief may be natural, it may be suggested or confirmed by phenomena, it may possess a history, it may long have influenced and inspired human thought ; and yet it may be so devoid of evidential support that, as soon as the light of truth is thrown upon it, it disappears and the world hears of it no more. This was the case (to take an obvious example) of the belief in the motion of the sun around the earth. No belief could be more natural or credible, none possessed a longer history, none had been made the basis of a larger scientific system; and yet of no belief has the surrender been more complete.

Is it, or ought it to be, with the belief in Immortality as it has been with the belief in the motion of the sun around the earth?

In default of evidence a belief so vital as that of Immortality cannot justly be regarded as a potent, still less as a paramount, motive of human conduct.

But it has been laid down that in the field of Theology the evidences which it is fair or sufficient to demand are not such as establish a proof, but such as establish a probability. The probability may be higher or lower, more or less cogent; but it is all that is attainable, and while it remains, it rightly affects and determines action. In matters upon which certainty is impossible, *i.e.*, in the vast majority of human interests and speculations, if there are nineteen arguments on one side, and twenty arguments of equal validity on the other, it is the part of prudence to act in accordance with the more numerous arguments, even though the numerical superiority be but one. And the prudential rule is not less clear, but indeed clearer, when the action is not some particular isolated incident, which cannot largely or permanently affect our personal welfare, but the greatest of all human interests, viz., the conduct of life. For in proportion as the issue is more serious, so is the duty and the importance of being on the safe side.

Yet again, it is one thing to surrender a false belief, or a belief which has been shown to be possibly false, for a true belief; it is another thing to surrender it for a mere negation. Human nature is so constituted that the absence of belief exercises a paralysing effect in some matters upon the intellectual, and in others upon the spiritual, faculty of Man. As it is his privilege to inquire, so it is equally his privilege to believe; and bad as error is, indifference or suspense of judgment may be worse. Thus the doctrine of the sun's motion itself was not upset merely by difficulty or disproof, it yielded to a more convincing doctrine. Men ceased to believe in the motion of the sun because they came to believe in the motion of the earth. It is not impossible that this belief may itself in its turn become merged in a larger generalisation. The law of the human intellect is that truer beliefs succeed, as the ages pass, to less true beliefs. Falsehood or error is supplanted by truth; it is not supplanted by negation.

Now the Immortality of the soul, if it is not proved, is at least not disproved by Philosophy or Science. It seems in its nature to be incapable of disproof. For the life of the soul transcends human observation. We know not whence it comes or whither it goes. It may be said that there is little or nothing to show the survival of the soul after death. I do not admit that it is so, but it may be so said. At all events, there is nothing to show the dissolution of the soul in death. Death is still the great mystery, the great possibility. It still hides its secret; but no one has the right to assert or assume that that secret, when it is revealed, will be found to be nothingness. The experience of discovery has constantly revealed new and living wonders in the physical universe and in the microcosm which is called Man. Why should death prove the sole disappointment? Why should it be assumed to be entirely dark and void?

This is the thought so beautifully suggested in Blanco White's celebrated sonnet:—

> "Mysterious Night! When our first parent knew
> Thee from report divine, and heard thy name,
> Did he not tremble for this lovely frame,
> This glorious canopy of light and blue?
> Yet 'neath a curtain of translucent dew,
> Bathed in the rays of the great setting flame,
> Hesperus with the host of heaven came,
> And lo! creation widened in Man's view.
> Who could have thought such darkness lay concealed
> Within thy beams, O Sun, or who could find
> Whilst fly and leaf and insect stood revealed,
> That to such countless orbs thou mad'st us blind?
> Why do we then shun death with anxious strife?
> If light can thus deceive, wherefore not life?"

At the worst Man is entitled to cherish the hope, if not, indeed, the faith, of an Immortal Life. The arguments of the sceptical philosophers from Lucretius in the *de Rerum Naturâ*—that extraordinary poetical and philosophical paradox—to Hume in his posthumous *Essay on the Immortality of the Soul* may be held (I do not say rightly) to diminish, in more or less degree, the probability of the soul's immortal being. But they leave it a possibility, and not so only, but a possibility with all the riches of hope and longing that are centred in the unknown. Immortality remains the open field of speculative and religious aspiration. Where science pauses, thought and devotion enter within the open grave.

But the disproof that Immortality can be disproved is not all that human nature expects. Even if it be granted, as it must be, that an Immortal Life remains, after all that can be said against it, a legitimate hope; even if it be granted, as it may be, that faith and piety are entitled to fill in the vacant spaces of such a hope with beliefs or vaticinations emanating from the conception of God, it is natural to ask not only why Immortality cannot justly be denied, but why it ought to be or may be embraced as a spiritual positive truth. The insufficiency of negative evidence does not make amends for the lack of such evidence as is positive or conclusive. He who would stake all upon the belief that life is immortal will desire to give a reason for the belief that is in him.

What, then, in nature and substance are the evidences which may be adduced for a belief in the Immortality of the soul?

They would seem to be broadly distinguishable as of two kinds. One part of them may be called external, the other internal evidences. It is necessary to exhibit the character of the two kinds.

It is possible to argue for Immortality from such phenomena as lie outside the soul itself. Thus there may be, *e.g.*, considerations of the nature of

Man or of the Nature of God, or, again, of the moral system and order of the Universe, which forbid or discourage the anticipation that the individual soul, after its association with the body, will be lost in nothingness. Indeed it is difficult to frame any complete or consistent theory of the relation of God to His Universe and to Man especially, as the highest known intellectual and moral being existent in it, without in some way speculating upon the future of Man and of that part of Man which is felt to be highest in him, viz., the spirit or soul. And the Universe is rich in analogies, which have been regarded, rightly or wrongly, as shedding light upon the probable destiny of Man. Such considerations are, as is clear, different in themselves and of different degrees of efficacy or validity; it is perhaps inevitable that they should be variously estimated by various minds; but the special note or character of all is that they depend upon some other evidence than a study of the soul itself. They are considerations drawn from without, not from within the soul. As being such, they are *external* evidences.

But it is equally possible to argue for Immortality from a consideration of the soul as it is in itself. Thus if it should appear that the soul, considered in itself, exhibits such essential characteristics as necessarily preclude, or even have generally and legitimately been felt to preclude, the idea of dissolution or to render it exceedingly improbable, no argument for Immortality could well be more weighty or decisive than that. And if it should appear that these characteristics of the soul, although no one of them may be logically conclusive, yet are numerous and concordant and impressive, and tend with increasing persistency to one end, then there would be an accumulation of such reasonable assurances as may be held to justify, upon stronger logical grounds than before, a belief in the Immortality which awaits the human soul when emancipated by death. And these considerations are native to the soul itself; they arise from a study of the soul apart from other existences; they are independent of theories respecting God or Man or the Universe; they are, in a word, the *internal* evidences of Immortality.

The present chapter will be concerned in the main with the external, the next with the internal evidences.

It must be admitted that the evidences, whether of one kind or the other, are not all of equal or nearly equal value. But, as has been already said, it must not be assumed that the evidences of one kind are superior to those of the other, or that the strength of the evidences as a whole is that of the weakest link in the chain. In a cumulative chain of evidence it is the strongest rather than the weakest link which gives character to the whole. The combination and correlation of multiple arguments creates a validity which no single argument possesses.

We will take first the evidences which have been called *external*.

And here it is necessary at the outset to put aside the argument, as it is termed, from analogy.

The strength of analogical argument is often misunderstood, especially in reference to such a doctrine as Immortality.

Analogy is not proof, it is illustration. It does not create belief, but it recommends and enforces belief, when already created. It depends for its validity upon the hypothesis, which may itself be the conclusion of a syllogism, that the phenomena between which analogy exists, or is taken as existing, are on the same plane, *i.e.*, that they are or may be results of the same creative energy, and so are or may be expressions of the same Master Mind.

The argument from analogy (though it is not

strictly an argument) is seen to perfection in the parables of Our Lord. But His parables are not logical premises from which a conclusion is derived. They are illustrations of the truths which He taught "as one having authority." Our Lord never argued, He never used proof; He took for granted such primary articles of religion as the Being of God, Providential Care, the probationary character of this life, the eternity of the life beyond the grave. And these articles of religion He sought to recommend by illustrations drawn from the common natural world. The sowing of the seed, the ripening of the harvest, the wheat and the tares, the grain of mustard seed, the draw-net, the lost sheep on the mountains—these and other stories like these are not demonstrations of novel and difficult truths; they are analogies or illustrations, and their influence upon the minds of millions of men has been the more powerful, as illustration comes home to men's consciences with a stronger and more impressive force than argument. To treat the analogy as an argument is to expose it to the shafts of acute criticism. It is to mistake the spires and pinnacles of belief for its foundations. For the force of an analogy in spiritual things is simply this : That if the same God is the Author of the natural and the spiritual worlds, it is not improbable, but may rather be expected, that a certain likeness—a certain conformity—should be observable in the phenomena of both worlds.

It would be wrong, then, to exaggerate the importance of the argument from analogy as an evidence of the soul's Immortality. Instances such as the emergence of the butterfly from the chrysalis, or the ripening of the grain from the buried seed, or the revival of the tree in the springtide after its seeming death in winter, are valuable, not so much as arguments, but as illustrations; they are designed as the supports of a belief already held on other grounds. The utmost that such illustrations can do is to remove what may have been felt as an *a priori* improbability; and this they may do, although the illustration is not exact or precise, but is, as every analogy must be, at the best only approximate to the truth which it is taken to exemplify. But the more convincingly it is brought home to thoughtful minds that all phenomena of life and nature are parts of one plan, the greater will be the readiness to admit the possibility and even the probability of developments of the soul beyond the narrow limits of space and time.

As the value of analogy in religious speculation is now in question, it will be well to consider the famous chapter—the 15th of the First Epistle to the Corinthians—in which St. Paul is believed to argue for the resurrection of the human body. So many tender and sacred associations cling to this chapter, that its logical importance has been often misunderstood. It has been called an incontrovertible proof of the resurrection of the body. But if it be treated as proof, it may easily be controverted. Why (it may be said) should the existence of different orders of created beings such as men and animals and birds and fishes, or of celestial luminaries differing in splendour as the sun and moon and stars, why should even the germination of the corn that springs from the bare grain constitute a proof that the human body, when laid in the tomb, will spontaneously emerge not into life only, but into a life far more glorious and sublime than the life of earth ?

As an argument, if such it were meant to be, the chapter would fail; as an analogy it is suggestive and inspiring. The thought underlying St. Paul's words is that Nature as the expression of Divine Intelligence exhibits everywhere a rich and progressive variety. In other words, it is that everywhere the distinction between the lower forms of life and the higher, and the passing of the lower into the higher, are the laws which operate in the Universe. He who denies, then, the resurrection, or, as St. Paul would rather call it, the glorification of the human body, sets an arbitrary limit to Omnipotence in the sphere in which Omnipotent Energy may be naturally expected to work with the highest result. And when the variety of form or splendour is admitted as a possibility, then analogies serve to illustrate what it may be or how it may take effect. Thus the contrast of the buried seed and the living grain is not a proof that the body which is laid in the tomb will rise to new life; but it is a suggestion that the new life may be a reality, and that, when it is realised, it may be infinitely more glorious than the old. In an argument from analogy all depends upon the point of view. To the darkened and confined vision of paganism, as is seen in the pathetic lines of Moschus, the new birth of the flowers in the springtide suggested no hope for Man, but only a deeper despair; so far worse was his destiny than theirs.

"Ah me, when the mallows wither in the garden

and the green parsley and the curled tendrils of the anise, on a later day they live again and spring in another year; but we men, we, the great and mighty or wise, when once we have died, in hollow earth we sleep, gone down into silence; a right long and endless and unawakening sleep." [1]

But to St. Paul's eye all Nature was eloquent of faith in the high immortal destiny of Man. "So also is the resurrection of the dead. It is sown in corruption; it is raised in incorruption: it is sown in dishonour; it is raised in glory: it is sown in weakness; it is raised in power: it is sown a natural body; it is raised a spiritual body." [2] "The body of our humiliation," "the body of Christ's glory," are, as it were, the poles of Man's corporeal destiny. The one is ours now; the other (in St. Paul's view) shall be ours hereafter. And "the body of His glory," is as much superior to "the body of our humiliation," as is the golden corn in the harvest-field to the bare grain cast into the earth, or the sun

---

[1] αἰ, αἰ, ταὶ μαλάχαι μὲν ἐπὰν κατὰ κᾶπον ὅλωνται
ἢ τὰ χλωρὰ σέλινα τό τ' εὐθαλὲς οὖλον ἀνήθον
ὕστερον αὖ ζώοντι καὶ εἰς ἔτος ἄλλο φύοντι·
ἄμμες δ'οἱ μεγάλοι καὶ καρτεροὶ ἢ σοφοὶ ἄνδρες
ὑππότε πρᾶτα θάνωμες, ἀνάκοοι ἐν χθονὶ κοιλᾷ
εὕδομες εὖ μαλὰ μακρὸν ἀτέρμονα νήγρετον ὕπνον·

[2] 1 Corinthians xv. 42-44.   (The Translation is Lang's.)

shining in his might to the most distant asteroid, or Man himself, the lord of creation, to the lowest animal.

Such is St. Paul's analogy, used to express the nature of the spiritual body. The analogies used in support of the Immortal Life are similar to it. They depend upon a belief in God as the Omnipotent Author of the world, whether temporal or moral or spiritual. Apart from that belief they claim no significance. But when that belief is granted, it renders a man's view of the Universe penetrating and spiritualising, so that he sees "more things in heaven and earth" than philosophy dreams of.

From the analogical teaching of our Lord and of St. Paul we may pass by a natural descent to Bishop Butler's celebrated work: *The Analogy of Natural and Revealed Religion to the Constitution and Course of Nature*. The *Analogy* must be read as it is. It must not be taken as a general defence of religion. It postulates the highest of all beliefs, the belief in God. It elaborates a comparison between religion, whether natural or revealed, on the one hand, and the phenomena of Nature on the other; but the comparison possesses no evidential value except upon the hypothesis that the phenomena of Nature represent the thought of a single Supreme Intelligence.

To treat the *Analogy* otherwise is to deal unfairly with it. Pitt is credited with the saying that it started more difficulties than it solved. As an argument, standing by itself, it may well create difficulties. But as an exposition of certain facts addressed to persons who accepted and asserted a particular theory of certain other facts, it holds a permanent place in theological controversy. It must be studied in relation to the deistical controversy of Bishop Butler's day. He himself states in the Preface what was its purpose, and it is strange that that purpose should have been misconceived.

With the strictly controversial side of the *Analogy* we are not here concerned. We shall see presently how it bears upon the great doctrine supported in this Essay. All that is necessary here is to emphasise the nature of the argument which Bishop Butler urges as analogical, viz., that where two sets or bodies of phenomena are severally regarded as expressions of the same Will, the characteristics which are admitted to occur in the one may be reasonably expected to occur in the other. And conversely that, where two sets of phenomena exhibit the same or similar characteristics, they may be reasonably referred to the same Will. And what is true of Bishop Butler's great *Analogy* is true of all analogies upon religion. It is when a truth has been already rendered probable or not improbable that analogy corroborates and confirms it.

It would seem, however, that writers upon Immortality have sometimes done their cause an injury by the stress they have laid upon necessarily inadequate analogical examples of a life transcending and transforming apparent death. They have cited the revivals or resurrections of Nature as affording evidence of a life after death; and when it has been shown that there is no such thing in Nature as a resurrection of the dead, when it has been shown that the seed, though buried, is not dead, and, not being dead, does not come to life again, the evidence in which they put their trust sinks under their feet. It is a different matter when the resurrections of Nature are treated as figurative; for then, however critically they may be scrutinised, they remain as figures, and their spiritual significance is unimpaired.

The analogies of Nature, then—the serpent, the butterfly upon Egyptian tombs, the seed of corn, the spring after winter—find their true place in a discussion of Immortality, not as establishing it as a truth, but as illustrating and enforcing it when it has been brought by argument into the region of probability. They are not proofs, but in a sense they are stronger or more persuasive than any proofs; for simile or analogy has a strange force in the world, and the minds of men lie naturally disposed to welcome the hypothesis of a great formative and comprehensive Providence.

But it is time to treat of the external evidences (as I have ventured to call them) for the doctrine of Immortality.

These evidences, if I do not mistake them, are threefold; not indeed that they can be absolutely distinguished, but that it is practically convenient so to distinguish them.

They lie severally in the constitution of the Universe, in the nature of Man, and in the Being of God.

From each of these three principles converging lights are shed upon the destiny of the soul. The lights are partial and imperfect, but they are not insufficient as evidences.

I propose to take them in order.

I. Evidence from the constitution of the Universe. The Immortality of the soul may be a philosophical or scientific as well as a religious doctrine. Although it has been adopted, as it were, by religion and enriched and ennobled by the wealth of religious sentiment and emotion, yet it may be, and sometimes has been, the result of intellectual speculation upon the phenomena of the natural world. The ancient thinkers who believed the doctrine of Immortality held it as an article not of religion but of philosophy. For in fact philosophy was the religion of Greece and Rome. The philosophers were the priests. The ministers of religion were mere hierophants; they were occupied in performing stated ceremonies; they chanted litanies, offered sacrifices and interpreted auguries; it was not their office (unless in the Eleusinian or other mysteries) to illumine the darkness of human conduct and human destiny. The divorce between religion and belief or conduct was complete. Cicero, in his *De Officiis*, a treatise upon the moral conduct of life, appeals to many motives and disciplines but hardly at all to religion. The only teachers of religion were the philosophers. There is a curious passage of Dio Chrysostom in which he says that, if a person were in anxiety or distress, he would send for a philosopher to give him comfort.[1]

[1] Dio Chrysostom, Orat., xxvii. p. 529.

It is in philosophy, then, that Greek thought exhibits its first signs of longing for arguments on behalf of Immortality. Philosophy laid the foundation of the great belief which religion has appropriated as its own.

It is impossible within the limits of this essay to summarise the reasonings of the Greek philosophers upon the destiny of the soul. But it is needless; for a single treatise—the *Phædo* of Plato—denotes the high-water mark of Greek religious philosophy. Whatever Greek imagination or reflexion could teach about the soul is found there.

The modern student of the *Phædo* is more deeply impressed by the strength of the belief to which it testifies than by the arguments underlying and supporting that belief. The serene confidence of Socrates in the presence of death is more cogent than any logical process. For the *Phædo* is argument touched with poetry and beautified by sanctity; and intellectual criticism falls to the ground at the spectacle of the philosopher spending his last hours, with his sorrowing friends gathered around him and the young disciple whom he loved sitting at his feet, in speculating upon the future of his soul in that unknown world for which his whole life had, as he deemed, been a preparation, and to which he would pass at the setting of the sun.

But the philosophical arguments of the *Phædo* deserve to be considered in the light of modern discovery. Socrates or Plato, like Lucretius, was gifted with the faculty of anticipating (if only by a suggestive intimation) the theories of an age far later than his own. In the *Phædo* he goes beyond intimations; he developes a theory of the Universe. The late Master of Balliol says with justice that his reasoning, if it be interpreted with a sense of true historical perspective, is the reasoning of philosophers to-day. Thus the argument drawn in the *Phædo* from the cycle of existence is a counterpart to the modern argument of the conservation of energy. Socrates asserts as a scientific principle that "opposites are generated out of their opposites," taking as examples of opposites not only relative terms like "greater" and "less," "stronger" and "weaker," "better" and "worse," but such processes as growing hot and cold, waking and sleeping; he argues that each one of these opposites passes into the other, the greater, *e.g.*, becoming the less and the less the greater, that which is awake falling asleep and that which is asleep awaking, and so on; this transition, then, is a law of Nature and, as it is evident that the living die, it is a proper inference that the dead return to life. And so "we arrive at the conclusion that the living come from the dead, just as the dead come from the living; and this, if true, affords a most certain proof that the souls of the dead exist in some place out of which they come again."[1]

Socrates holds, then, that all existence moves in a cycle, from life to death and then again from death to life. He contends, too, that this movement is eternal; it is ceaseless change, it is never destruction. Thus the Immortality of the soul is a supreme instance of a law universal in Nature. As day succeeds to night, and motion to rest, so life is the sequel of death.

It must be admitted that Socrates gives no adequate proof of the cyclical movement upon which he bases his belief in the soul's Immortality; it is in part a poetical fancy, in part a scientific generalisation, in part a mere playing with words. But it is a witness to the philosophical difficulty of believing that whatever has come into being can be lost. And that this is his meaning is clear; for he adds that, unless the process of mutual generation were

[1] *Phædo*, p. 72A.

to take place, all things would ultimately be reduced to a stagnant uniformity.

This is not the sole Socratic argument for Immortality, but it is the only one which may be said to fall under the constitution of the Universe.

In modern thought the doctrine of the cycle disappears; it is replaced by the doctrine of continuity. All force, as all matter, is perpetual. The law of conservation holds good throughout Nature. "There is no such thing," it has been said, "as annihilation. Things are changed, transformations abound, but essences do not cease to be."[1]

The natural expectation of the soul's Immortality may be put in these words :—

Human nature (it may be said) consists of two parts, body and soul; these two parts are the constituent elements of human nature; they are evidently separated in death. But the fate of the body, after this separation, is ascertained; it is dissolved but not destroyed, it undergoes certain chemical and physical changes, but it does not cease to be; and if it be so, the inference is that the soul is not destroyed at death, but experiences a change similar perhaps to that of the body or

[1] Alger, *A Critical History of the Doctrine of a Future Life*, p. 42.

different from it, but at all events a change which leaves it still and always an entity.

All that is now urged is that the law of conservation holds good, as in the body, so in the soul. Some philosophers have made a distinction between body and soul in respect of their liability, not indeed to destruction, but to dissolution. Thus Clarke, in replying to Dodswell, used this language: "As evidently as the known properties of matter prove it to be certainly a discerpible substance, whatever other unknown properties it may be endued with, so evidently the known and confessed properties of immaterial beings prove them to be indiscerpible, whatever unknown properties they may be endued with."[1] And no doubt, whether Clarke's view be accepted or not, it would be a mistake to press the parallelism of soul and body in respect of their future destiny beyond due limit; for there is as yet nothing to suggest that the soul, if it survives the event of death, will, like the body, experience dissolution.

It will, however, be time to consider the probable fate of the soul when we come to examine the

---

[1] A Letter to Mr. Dodswell, p. 101, quoted by Mr. Gladstone in the *North American Review* for January, 1896, p. 6.

evidence for Immortality which lies in the nature of the soul itself. If Clarke's view be just, it constitutes an argument *à fortiori*. For if the soul differs from the body, in that it is immaterial and therefore indiscerpible (to use Clarke's word) and if the body, although being discerpible, is not destroyed or destructible in death, it is abundantly clear that destruction is not and cannot be the destiny of the soul itself in death.

But the argument derivable from the constitution of the Universe holds good, whatever view be taken of the soul. It is that nothing is destroyed; everything is changed, but nothing destroyed; and therefore the soul survives the great change known as death.

That this argument, taken by itself, constitutes a probability of the soul's permanent being, it is, in my opinion, difficult, if not indeed impossible, to doubt. That probability, like others relating to the soul, is no doubt affected and strengthened by the belief in God. But, even apart from such belief, annihilation is so strongly opposed to the apparent and ascertained laws of the universe that it is certainly more difficult of acceptance on scientific grounds than any theory of the soul's Immortality.

What are the conditions of the soul's surviving

existence is a question which will come under review in the last chapter. Natural Religion may suggest the fact of Immortality; but it does not, except within narrow limits, suggest its conditions. If upon these any authoritative voice is heard in the world, it can be no other than the voice of Revelation.

But Natural Religion, which is only another name for devout Philosophy, recommends, if it does not enforce, a belief in the soul's Immortality. For without any question of spiritual continuity or development, or reward and punishment, or the laws of immaterial being, Natural Religion justly asks how it is scientific or philosophical or legitimate in speculation to assume as certain or even as probable that the principle of conservation, which is universal as the Universe itself, should fail, when there is no proof whatever of its failing, in the life of the individual human soul.

This is the argument for Immortality from the constitution of the Universe.

But the argument lies open to certain difficulties which it would not be reasonable to ignore.

And of these the most interesting, as it is the most important, is the question of the bearing of such evidence as the constitution of the Universe affords for the Immortality of individual human souls upon the probable future destiny of the lower animals.

To some minds it will seem that an argument for Immortality loses dignity or importance if it applies to the lower animals as cogently as to Man; to others it will seem that such an argument as the law of conservation necessarily embraces all forms of energy or vitality.

But it is impossible to reflect upon Immortality, especially as attested by a law of the Universe, without inquiring, Is it probable in the light of the considerations adduced for human Immortality that the souls of the lower animals, if they possess souls, are capable of an immortal existence like the souls of men? or in other words, Is it reasonable to believe, and does the constitution of the Universe recommend the belief, that, whatever be the fate of human beings after death, the same or similar will be or may be the fate of the animals?

Nobody who has pondered the probabilities of Immortality will offer a reply to this question without a feeling of diffident humility.

The possible Immortality of the lower animals is not a speculation that can be put aside as unphilosophical. It is true that human thought, oscillating, as its habit is, between extremes, has tended at one time to disparage, and at another to exaggerate, the similarities of the human and the lower animal natures. The philosophical school of which Descartes was the head looked upon the animals as mere machines or automata. But Descartes, it seems, was led to take this view of the animals just because he denied that animals could have souls. Considering the soul to be an entity independent of the body, though temporarily allied to it, and considering animals to possess no soul, he could only classify them with mechanical instruments. But that has not been the view of some of the most profound among the thinkers whether in ancient or in modern times, nor does it seem to be the view which naturally arises in the human mind, when the doctrine of Immortality is first conceived as a positive truth.

Most people are familiar with Pope's lines:

> "Lo! the poor Indian whose untutored mind
> Sees God in clouds and hears Him in the wind.
> . . . .
> To be contents his natural desire;
> He asks no angel's wing, no seraph's fire,
> But thinks admitted to that equal sky
> His faithful dog shall bear him company."[1]

---

[1] *Essay on Man*, i. 99, *sqq.*

But it is not always recognised that this is held by anthropologists to be the natural presumption or intuition of the human mind. Immortality, wherever it is believed among primitive men, is nowhere and never looked upon as a distinction between Man and the lower animals. Savages generally believe that the spirit or soul survives the grave; but they believe it of all spirits and souls, not of human souls only; they do not conceive that the souls of men should be endowed with a futurity, and the souls of the other animals should not. "The sense of an absolute psychical distinction between man and beast, so prevalent in the civilised world, is hardly to be found among the lower races." [1]

As sometimes happens in religious philosophy, the thought of cultivated and enlightened men even in a late age has visibly tended in this special instance to coincide with the intuition of primitive mankind. No doubt it may be alleged that it was the poverty of the conception of the soul even in human beings which led the savage, and it is the dignity of that conception even in the animals which leads the philosopher, to postulate or anticipate for both the

[1] Tylor, *Primitive Culture*, vol. i. p. 469.

same destiny. But, whatever the cause may be, the fact remains. Let me refer to two passages chosen from master-thinkers, one of the old classical, the other of the modern Christian world.

The *Republic* of Plato ends with the story of Er, the son of Armenius, who, twelve days after that he was believed to have been slain in battle, came to life again upon the funeral pyre and related what he had seen in the world below. He told how the souls of men and women after purification were permitted to make choice of new lives, "and not only did men pass into animals, but I must also mention (he said) that there were animals tame and wild who changed into one another and into corresponding human natures—the good into the gentle and the evil into the savage, in all sorts of combinations."[1]

Bishop Butler, in the chapter of the *Analogy* which relates to the future life, was led to consider the probable destiny of the lower animals. And although he expresses himself with reserve, still the fact that he replies to objections alleged against their Immortality is an evidence of his mental inclination; for he concludes that "all difficulties as to the manner how they are to be disposed of

[1] Book x. p. 620 D.

are so apparently and wholly founded on our ignorance, that it is wonderful they should be insisted upon by any but such as are weak enough to think they are acquainted with the whole system of things." [1]

The names of Plato and Butler stand upon the high mountain-chain of human thought. It were easy to add to them other names, such as those of Leibnitz or Coleridge or Agassiz; for all these thinkers and others like them have advocated, though on different grounds and by different reasonings, the Immortality of all living creatures. Nor can it be urged that it is a doctrine which has been ever felt to be prohibited by the Christian Revelation. Mr. Wesley, in his famous sermon [2] on the 8th chapter of the Epistle to the Romans, after describing the suffering and humiliation of the animals, uses these words: "Will 'the creature'—will even the brute creation always remain in this deplorable condition? God forbid that we should affirm this; yea, or even entertain such a thought! While 'the whole creation groaneth together' (whether men attend or not), their groans are not

---

[1] Part i. chap. i.
[2] Sermon lx. The whole sermon is wonderfully interesting and instructive.

dispersed in idle air, but enter into the ears of Him that made them. While His creatures 'travail together in pain,' He knoweth all their pain, and is bringing them nearer and nearer to the birth, which shall be accomplished in its season. He seeth 'the earnest expectation' wherewith the whole animated creation waiteth for that final 'manifestation of the sons of God,' in which 'they themselves also shall be delivered' (not by annihilation, annihilation is not deliverance) from the present 'bondage of corruption into' a measure of 'the glorious liberty of the children of God.'

"Nothing can be more express—away with vulgar prejudices, and let the plain word of God take place. They 'shall be delivered from the bondage of corruption into glorious liberty'—even a measure according as they are capable—of the 'liberty of the children of God.'

"To descend to a few particulars. The whole brute creation will then, undoubtedly, be restored not only to the vigour, strength, and swiftness which they had at their creation, but to a far higher degree of each than they ever enjoyed. They will be restored, not only to that measure of understanding which they had in Paradise, but to a degree of it as much higher than that as the understanding of an elephant is beyond that of a worm. And whatever affections they had in the garden of God, will be restored with vast increase, being exalted and refined in a manner which we ourselves are now not able to comprehend. The liberty they then had will be completely restored, and they will be free in all their motions. They will be delivered from all irregular appetites, from all unruly passions, from every disposition that is either evil in itself, or has any tendency to evil. No rage will be found in any creature, no fierceness, no cruelty, or thirst for blood. So far from it, that 'the wolf shall dwell with the lamb, the leopard shall lie down with the kid, the calf and the young lion together; and a little child shall lead them. The cow and the bear shall feed together; and the lion shall eat straw like the ox. They shall not hurt nor destroy in all my holy mountain.'"

It may be interesting to ask what has been the influence of modern scientific theory upon Man's view of his relation to the lower animals.

In one conspicuous respect it has intensified the sense of kinship or affinity between them. For the Darwinian theory, which is now accepted in some form or other by all scientific thinkers as the most reasonable account of physiological facts, insists that Man, in his corporeal nature, is, if not descended from, yet intimately connected with, some lower form of animal life. This speculation has not, I think, produced as strong an effect as might have been anticipated in the quickening of human sympathy among Darwinians for the sufferings and disabilities of the animals. Nor again has it strengthened scientific belief in the future psychical or spiritual existence of the animals; it has rather impaired belief in the capacity of Man for such an existence. Darwin indeed spoke with his usual caution of his theory as affecting the probable fate of human souls. "Few persons," he says, "feel any anxiety from the impossibility of determining at what precise period in the development of the individual, from the first trace of a minute germinal vesicle, man becomes an immortal being, and there is no greater cause for anxiety because the period cannot possibly be determined in the gradually ascending organic scale." [1]

But some of his disciples have been less scrupulous than their master. Thus Carl Vogt has not

[1] *Descent of Man*, part iii. chap. xxi. p. 613.

hesitated to declare that "physiology pronounces definitely and categorically against the idea of individual Immortality, as indeed against all notions founded upon that of the independent existence of the soul."[1] He refers not to the souls of the lower animals alone, but to Man's soul. Such is the dogmatism which was once regarded as theological, but has descended from Theology to Science.

Yet while some scientific writers, in the name of Darwinism have insisted with a passionate earnestness upon the absolutely materialistic and positive conception of human or animal nature, there have been thinkers of higher tone and deeper insight who have keenly realised that no revelation of modern Science has destroyed or diminished the mystery attaching to the nature and destiny of the lower beings by which Man is surrounded and aided or harassed in his daily life. Cardinal Newman, for instance, has spoken of the lower animals as being in their nature and their destiny not less incomprehensible to Man's present intellectual insight than the very angels of whom Holy Scripture tells. And there are not a few Christians beside him who have sought to justify the proximity of the animals to mankind by

[1] Ueberweg, *History of Philosophy*, vol. ii. p. 332.

dignifying their character both in this life and after it.

The question remains, then, Are these mysterious beings mortal or immortal? We know so little of their life here; have they another life? And is it such as ours will be? They are like us, and yet unlike; near us, yet infinitely far; a pathos, as of defeat or failure, rests on their lives; what is to be said or imagined about their destiny?

This, at least, is sure, that neither Science nor Religion sets a bar to the belief or the hope of their Immortality. Nay, if the Immortality of the human soul is once admitted, it seems to follow that, in proportion as the lower animals are assimilated to Man in their physical or intellectual or moral nature, the probability of their sharing Man's Immortality, though under certain limiting conditions, is increased.

Christian Theology, it must be admitted, has been occupied too exclusively with the influence of Redemption upon Humanity. The truer view is that, as all creation, *i.e.*, every created thing, was mysteriously implicated in Man's Fall, so all creation is participant in his Redemption. St. Paul in many passages of his Epistles, but especially in the 8th chapter of his Epistle to the Romans, conceives not of Humanity alone, but of all creation as regenerated by the Incarnation of the Son of God. "The creature was made subject to vanity . . . the creature itself shall be delivered from the bondage of corruption into the glorious liberty of the children of God."

In the light of this conception it would seem natural that Immortality should be the prerogative of the lower animals as well as of Man, but that the Immortality of the lower animals should be conditioned by the limitations (whatever they may be) of their own nature. The lower animals, as being akin to Man, will inherit, like Man, an Immortality; but in so far as their nature may be said to fall below his, their Immortality will be less august and perfect than his.

If it is necessary then to put forth any hypothesis as to the future life of the lower animals, it is necessary to examine the constituent elements of human and of animal nature.

A spiritual Immortality cannot be the lot of such beings as are other than spiritual.

In the first chapter of this essay it was shown that human nature is composed of three parts or elements, viz., body, mind or soul, and spirit.

How far do these three elements appear in the lower animals?

The body ($\sigma\hat{\omega}\mu a$) Man shares with all created things. It is a part of plants as much as of animals, of the lower animals as much as of Man. It is dissolved at death; it is not essentially the heir of Immortality. Whether the Christian Revelation throws any light, and if so what is the light thus thrown, upon the future of the human body it will be time to consider hereafter. I am dealing now with such arguments only as are independent of any positive revelation. But the $\psi v\chi\acute{\eta}$, *i.e.*, the emotional and intellectual part of human nature which is properly to be called the "soul" as distinct from the "spirit," the lower animals share with Man, only not completely, but in a certain limited or conditional degree. That is to say, the emotional desires and the intellectual activities of the lower animals are not dissimilar to the human but inferior. It is self-evident that the lower animals are naturally incapable of the keen delights and pains awakened in Man by memory, hope, beauty, wonder, disappointment, enthusiasm, as they are incapable of the intellectual achievements which have laid the physical Universe open to his understanding. There is a third part of human nature, viz., the πνεῦμα, or spirit, by which Man, as has been said, attains to the knowledge of God ; and of this, although it is the supreme human faculty, the lower animals in their nature are devoid.

Assuming then, as has been argued in the first chapter, that the Immortality which is commonly called an Immortality of the soul ought in strict accuracy to be taken as an Immortality of the πνεῦμα and the ψυχή, *i.e.*, of the spiritual, intellectual and emotional parts of human nature, it would seem to follow that we are justified in believing the lower animals to survive their physical death, but to survive it in a condition of limited, although possibly progressive, intellectual and emotional capacity, but without any development of the spiritual faculty by which Man knows God. The Immortality of the lower animals, if so regarded, is not the same as Man's ; it lacks the special determining character of Man's Immortality ; and the conclusions at which it is possible to arrive respecting human destiny do not, except partially and incidentally, relate to the destiny of the lower animals. For as spirit (πνεῦμα) is higher than soul (ψυχή), so is Man's future higher than that of the lower animals.

It is the Immortality of Man which is the subject of this essay. And in Man it is not the ψυχή or soul only, nor even the ψυχή, although invested and enriched with all such prerogatives as establish the intellectual superiority of Man to the lower animals, but primarily and essentially the πνεῦμα or spiritual faculty which is the inheritor and recipient of Immortality. And hence it is, as will be more fully set forth afterwards, that the revelations of the unseen world generally represent Man as spending himself, as a spiritual being, in acts of worship; for no sooner is his spirit emancipated by death from the embarrassments and obscurations of the flesh than it expands and expatiates in devotion, as enjoying at last an unimpeded vision of God, contemplating His excellency with inextinguishable delight and losing all taint of earthly infirmity in the perfectness of adoration and love.

Still the considerations adduced for Man's Immortality from the apparent law of conservation in the Universe must be held to support, though with inferior emphasis, the Immortality of all living creatures.

But it is time to consider certain speculative difficulties affecting human Immortality itself.

The Eternal or Immortal Life, whatever its nature may be, is confessedly invisible. It is not a life that is subject to the sight or sense or perception. And there are minds which experience a difficulty in realising an invisible and intangible existence. I do not say that the difficulty is felt by such minds as have received a philosophical training; but a good many minds of men are not philosophical.

It is not, however, a strong or serious difficulty. There is no possibility of supposing, even after brief reflexion, that such phenomena as are cognisable by the senses are coextensive and coincident with the Universe of created things. If it were so, it would be irrational to believe in God. " No man hath seen God at any time." It would be irrational to believe in the world of angels or spirits. To believe in such a world is to believe (at least) in the possibility of a personal life invisible and yet immortal.

These are theological considerations, and their gravity is dependent upon a certain religious and even Christian attitude of mind, but apart from Christianity, apart from all religion, it is perspicuous that human senses are limited to a certain range, and beyond that range there is much that exists and operates, although it lacks the certificate of sensual testimony.

I am arguing now that the invisibility or imperceptibility of the spiritual and Immortal Life is no sufficient reason for disbelieving in it, if it be recommended to belief on reasonable grounds.

The senses of Man are but partial witnesses to truth. They are the instruments available for registering phenomena within a certain range or area, but not beyond it. That they do not register other phenomena is no proof that those phenomena do not exist; it is not even a proof that they cannot be known.

It is enough for my purpose to show the limitation of the senses; I do not now consider how it may be modified or corrected. Let me take two or three instances of this limitation.

The telescopic camera photographs innumerable worlds, but of these many are invisible to the human eye. The magnetic needle responds to impulsive forces which lie beyond the perceptivity of the most delicate and sensitive human nerves. Let there be less than thirty or more than four thousand vibrations of matter in a second, and the human ear is impotent to discern a tone. The seven colours of the rainbow fall within the perceptive power of human eyes; but all that lies beyond the violet is darkness. Is it to be imagined that there exist no tones or colours of which other beings than Man in other worlds by other faculties than ours might take cognisance?

The atomic theory is the basis of modern physics; but what is an atom? Who has seen it or can define it? The ethereal *medium* is a necessary postulate of the theory of light, but what positive proof of the ether exists? And to speak again of the animals, whose nature throws so much light not upon the dignity alone but upon the poverty of human endowments, it is probable that the mystery of animal life—so striking when it is pointed out, yet so often forgotten—is best interpreted (so far as it can be known at all) by the hypothesis that the lower animals see sights and hear sounds, and in general are capable of perceptions, which transcend the scope and capacity of human faculties.

Such considerations as these ally themselves to St. Paul's argument (which has already been set out) for the soul's Immortality from the infinite variety of the Universe. They may be said to justify or allow (and they need do no more) the belief in a sublime and sacred world although invisible, a world transcending human sense, a world Divine. And if it is possible and reasonable to believe in such a world as the home of human souls or human spirits, then it is enough to show that the belief itself is consonant with the general course or constitution of the Universe.

Let me put the argument from the constitution of the Universe in this way.

Nature, scientifically regarded, makes it probable that the individual soul is not destroyed by death. The constitution of Nature, so far as it is at present understood, leaves ample scope for a life independent of those conditions of time and space which regulate human existence in this world. The life of spirits centres in God who is Himself "Spirit." It participates, though not unrestrictedly, in the attributes of the Divine Being. It is a life without which the intellectual and moral laws of the Universe would lack completeness; for it would seem to follow, as a natural, if not indeed as a necessary inference, that if there are higher beings than Man whose life is invisible and yet immortal (for the angels of God, it is written, never die); and if there are lower beings too, such as the animals, whose life is material and transitory, in a sense in which

Man's is not, and incapable of a pure spirituality, then Man himself, as standing between the two orders of being should enjoy a prophetic vision, even in this life, of an invisible and Immortal Life in which he shall be exalted above his present limitation and shall behold the face of God.

This is the destiny, this the intrinsic dignity of Man.

We may pass, then, from the evidence of the Universe to consider the—

II. Evidence from the nature of Man.

The question is : Does human nature, considered in itself, afford any presumption of Man's Immortality ?

It will be understood that under the nature of Man is not here included the nature of the human soul itself. That will form the subject of consideration in the next chapter.

The constitution of the Universe is one thing; the place of Man within that constitution is another.

There may be discovered in the Universe general laws, such as the law of the indestructibility of matter or force called conservation, which make it not a difficulty, but a reasonable supposition, that the soul of Man should survive the experience known as death. That such a law exists, and that it tells in favour of Immortality, has been already argued.

Or, again, there may be discerned in the nature of Man himself such a character of proper dignity or perpetuity as suggests, if it does not compel, the supposition that his energy will not be limited to threescore years and ten.

It is the tacit or express conviction of such a dignity that has probably influenced thinkers, and Christian thinkers especially, to believe in the Immortality of the human soul, while they denied it, or did not assert it, in regard to the souls of the lower animals. But the truth or error of this supposition can only be determined, if at all, by the study of human nature in itself.

It is strange, as has been said, and yet pathetic, to observe how Man has been tempted at one time to exaggerate, and at another to depreciate, the dignity of his own personal nature. He has seemed to himself in history now a little lower than the angels, now a little higher than the beasts. Of late, perhaps in consequence of the Darwinian theory, the dominant note in his estimate of himself has been humility.

It is better in the interest of human virtue that

Man should take too high than too low a view of his own nature. But the truth can be learnt only by a study of human nature itself.

We have seen that it consists of three parts, viz., of body, soul, and spirit. We have seen that these parts are logically separable. We have seen that the spirit or spiritual faculty is the highest part in human nature. And we have seen that, in proportion as Man cultivates and elevates the spiritual part of his nature, he is assimilated to the Being of God.

It is evident then that, if any part of Man's composite nature is endowed with an essential Immortality, it is the spirit.

Conversely if there is any part which is essentially incapable of Immortality, it is the body.

But in life the spirit and the body (I do not now speak of the soul) are intimately and indissolubly united.

In death the union is dissolved.

It has been argued, as an argument against Immortality, that the dissolution of the union between spirit and body must involve the destruction of identity. If that argument were sound it would be fatal to the great belief for which I plead. But is it sound?

All depends upon the question of identity, and upon the way in which identity is affected by natural changes. It is not necessary to define in what identity consists; it is enough to show that a being may undergo great and critical vicissitudes of substance and form, and among them grave personal losses and diminutions as well as accretions, without sacrificing his identity.

Thus there is no doubt that the passing from infancy to boyhood or girlhood, and from these into the perfect state of manhood or womanhood, leaves the identity of the individual unimpaired. And this is so, although the physical or material part of Man's being, *i.e.*, his body, is constantly changing; it is scientifically held to undergo a complete change in some seven years. Yet a man speaks of himself as the same, and is the same, although no particle of his body remains unchanged. Identity, then, whatever it may strictly be, does not consist in the material substance of the body. In what, then, does it consist if not in the soul?

Again, the body may suffer grave losses and mutilations without any detriment to personality or identity. Thus a man who has lost his legs or arms or other parts of his body is still as much a human being, and is the same human being, as he was when he was physically perfect. It is evident that the dissolution or amputation of much, and perhaps of all, that is material and physical in human nature does not, or at least need not, imply the destruction of his being, or of that part of his being which constitutes himself, *i.e.*, his soul.

Bishop Butler, in the first chapter of the first part of his *Analogy* considers, as is well known, the question of identity in reference to the change actually or possibly effected by death. The conclusion to which he comes is important. "Our finding," he says, "that the dissolution of matter, in which living beings were most nearly interested, is not their dissolution, and that the destruction of several of the organs and instruments of perception and of motion belonging to them is not their destruction, shows demonstratively that there is no ground to think that the dissolution of any other matter, or destruction of any other organs and instruments, will be the dissolution or destruction of living agents from the like kind of relation. And we have no reason to think we stand in any other kind of relation to anything which we find dissolved by death."

If then the separability of the soul from the body, and its continuance in life after separation, is rendered possible as a belief by these and other similar considerations, it is borne out by the positive evidences of the soul's independent existence which lie within common experience. Such are the phenomena of dreams or waking visions, imagination, memory and consciousness. All these show or tend to show the reality of an intellectual, as well as of a spiritual, existence distinct from the bodily.

Such then is the primary argument for the possibility (to put it at the lowest) of the soul's survival after death and its Immortality. Death, like decay or disease, does not apparently affect what is necessary or vital to being; it affects the external attributes but not the essential nature of Man; it cannot therefore be held to imply dissolution or destruction of the man himself.

The phenomena of consciousness show the soul during life to be independent of the body. The soul or spirit asserts and exhibits itself during life in activities wholly distinct from the corporeal. And it is precisely these activities which are highest and purest and most widely removed from association with the body—wonder, enlightenment, rapture, devotion, adoration—that are believed to find their perfect sphere of exercise in the world that is invisible and immortal.

But this primary argument is only preparatory to the evidences which make the belief in Immortality reasonable or probable. For it may be true that physical decay or death does not necessarily imply the destruction of the soul, and yet that truth does not in itself establish a conviction of the soul's Immortality.

In any such conviction the study of human nature becomes important.

But that study raises the question of Man's legitimate place in the Universe. His place, if it can be ascertained, will afford grounds for an estimate of his destiny.

Man is not, it has been said, a good judge of his own nature. Yet he is the sole judge. He may be tempted to set his nature too high or too low, but he must pass judgment upon it, if he aspires to know himself.

It may be asked then : Does the nature of Man, impartially considered as far as it may be, suggest for him a destiny so august as a spiritual Immortality ?

It is not right, in any survey of human nature, to exaggerate the distinction between Man and the lower animals. Nor is it necessary; for the means of estimating Man's destiny lie in his nature as it is, not in the dignity of its origin or in a comparison between it and other natures. Whether it is immediately derived from the dust of the earth or from a lower form of animal life is not a consideration that affects the capacity of Man for the spiritual life in the present or the future.

But whatever be the origin of Man's nature, it remains true that Man is the climax of the visible creation. As the spirit is supreme among the elements of Man's nature, so is Man in his nature supreme among the multitude of created beings. There is a gradual evolutionary process from the lowest created being upwards to Man and among men to the highest Man. It is difficult to believe that at Man, *i.e.*, at human nature as it now is seen, the process stops short. Human nature contains within itself the promise of better things than now appear. Man looks beyond the present to futurity.

The superior dignity of Man to other creatures is so much added to the strength of the case for his Immortality. Whatever argument is adduced for the probable Immortality of the lower animals holds more than good for the Immortality of Man. If the constitution of the Universe, as has been suggested, leads to the belief or the supposition that those animals are immortal, that belief or supposition is greatly strengthened in the case of mankind. For it is Man's admitted superiority to the animals that has been regarded by philosophical thinkers in recent no less than in former days as one main proof of his Immortality. So Dr. Martineau says, "A higher destiny (than that of animals) is claimed for man, on the strength of his higher nature."[1] And Mr. Fiske, "To deny the everlasting persistence of the spiritual element in Man is to rob the whole process (*i.e.*, the process of evolution) of its meaning."[2] For indeed the Immortality of the soul or spirit of Man is, as it seems, the only probable consummation of the cosmical process which dominates the ages.

It is because Man is potentially so great in intellect and spirit, that he claims an immortal existence. To realise the greatness of Man is to realise his eternity. It follows that in proportion

[1] *A Study of Religion*, book iv. chap. i. vol. ii. p. 324.
[2] *The Destiny of Man*, p. 115.

to the elevation of a human character is the difficulty of believing it to be mortal. All the great and the good upon earth in all the ages have rendered to mankind this signal service, that they have exalted and amplified the hopes of human destiny. But among all Jesus Christ stands supreme. For He revealed before men's eyes a life so spiritual, so sacred, so Divine, that they who saw it knew it to be victorious over death. But of this life we shall speak in the last chapter. We refer to it here only because it seems that one reason why men are apt to doubt the doctrine of Immortality is that their own lives are poor, ignoble and earthbound. Could they but rise above themselves and their own circumstances, they would rise into the atmosphere of Immortality.

It is the religious life at its highest which postulates Immortality. The quality of sanctity forbids the idea of death. To know God is to anticipate the Divine life. When St. Paul was "caught up to the third heaven," and "heard unspeakable words which it is not lawful for a man to utter," he could no longer believe in his mortality. The Immortal Life, the life of one who had "risen with Christ," became to him an axiom of Theology.

But if the experiences and emotions of religion are, as indeed they are, the most powerful and convincing witnesses of Immortality, they are not the only witnesses. The rapture or enthusiasm of the saints suggests Immortality, as evincing the reality of faculties and sentiments which do not and cannot find satisfaction in this life. But human nature is rich in suggestions of the Unseen; for to no man are there lacking powers and occasions, many or few, when he becomes fully aware of the powers, which take him, as it were, out of himself, beyond himself, and make him participant in a life higher than his own.

Such intimations of Immortality lie in the realms of art, of poetry, of eloquence.

Art is not the mere imitation of Nature. It is the idealisation of Nature. Art is to Nature what the soul is to the body of Man. It is something sublime, ethereal, Divine, like beauty itself.

Among the arts there is none so spiritual as music. No art evokes results so wonderful by means so slender. None is so mysterious or so magical. None lifts Man so near to Heaven. How is it then that the simple notes of Music exercise this strange imperious spell? It is not in themselves; they are but the instruments to set free, as it were, from captivity the secret emotions and aspirations of the soul. They reveal Man to himself, by exalting him above himself.

Nor is it to music alone, though to music in the highest degree, that this strange influence belongs. The masterpieces of art, the intuitions of poetry, the supreme efforts of eloquence, are all alike capable of lifting the soul, though for a brief space, into a higher life and a grander sphere than the terrestrial.

And something of the same effect is seen in those rare moments when a man transcends the narrow interests by which his life is too often and painfully fettered, when he knows that not in self-love, but in self-sacrifice and devotion does his true good lie. For the heroisms and sanctities of life are, as it were, attestations of a kinship with Divinity. Of this spiritual kinship Wordsworth's poetry affords the most natural and beautiful expression. Thus it is when he writes:

> "Enough if something from our hands have power
> To live and act and serve the future hour,
> And if as tow'rd the silent tomb we go
> Through love, through hope and faith's transcendent dower,
> We feel that we are greater than we know." [1]

---

[1] *The River Duddon. Afterthought.*

But it is in the *Ode on the Intimations of Immortality* that Wordsworth's teaching attains to its highest point. That teaching has often been compared to the doctrine of 'Ανάμνησις or Reminiscence which is used by Socrates in the *Phædo* as one of his reasons for anticipating the Immortality of the soul. Yet at first sight the contrast seems greater than the similarity. For while Plato rests his plea for Immortality upon a process of remembering, Wordsworth rests his upon a process of oblivion.

"Our birth is but a sleep and a forgetting."

Yet there is a deeper sense in which the poet and the philosopher are at one. For alike they make their appeal to an intuition, a knowledge beyond the range of experience, and to that knowledge as lifting Man above the things of earth. That such teaching implies the pre-existence even more than the present or future existence of the soul is a thought common to both, and it is a thought which will claim consideration, but not here. All that need now be said is that, if there be something in Man which has caught glimpses of a supernatural glory, if it be true, as the poet tells, that

> " Not in entire forgetfulness,
> And not in utter nakedness,
> But trailing clouds of glory do we come
> From God who is our home "

then that something is eternal, it is Divine.

Thus the highest teachings of the old world and of the new agree in their witness to that mystery of human nature (as I have ventured to call it), that greater something than earthly greatness which is in Man the evidence of the Divine.

It was not in Wordsworth's view to dwell upon the witness of the conscience. Yet conscience is a prophetic part of human nature; it is a sanctuary within Man, and it attests his affinity to God. I cannot think of conscience solely as the product of accumulated earthly experiences. It speaks with an authority higher than of earth. It is the voice of God. And as being such it points, like other high endowments of Man, only with an emphasis to which no other endowment attains, to Man's unique character and to his immortal destiny.

For all the faculties and capacities of Man which have been enumerated, reaching out as they do beyond the present or material life into the spiritual regions of Eternity, are so many indications and intimations of the future which awaits him when he shall be emancipated from the flesh.

From such witnesses of Immortality it is natural to pass to what has been theologically termed the *argumentum ab appetitu æternitatis, i.e.,* the argument that Man is immortal because he naturally and intensely desires Immortality.

We have to consider the value or cogency of that argument.

It has been already shown that human nature instinctively shrinks from the prospect of annihilation. But is the wish for Immortality a proof of it?

All depends, it would seem, upon the motive underlying the wish.

The argument for Immortality from the mere desire of it is easily misunderstood. Young, the author of the *Night Thoughts,* put it in this bald form:

"Who wishes life immortal proves it too."

But to say that a mere wish is a proof that the wish will be granted is to put a weapon into the hand of the sceptics. We wish for many things in this life and do not gain them. Why should we assume that a wish will be gratified just because it refers to the future life? If we may argue at all from this world to the next, we must argue that the unknown will be like the known. We cannot argue that a want of which we are conscious in the known world will become a satisfaction in the unknown.

The absurdity of the inference drawn from Man's desire to his destiny has been exhibited by numerous writers, and among modern writers especially by Hume in his posthumous *Essay upon Immortality*, and by Hume's exponent, the late Professor Huxley. But all depends, as has been said, upon the motive of the wish.

What is it that makes men yearn for Immortality?

The desire is plainly not a mere selfish appetite. We do not desire Immortality for ourselves alone, we desire it for others; nay, we desire it more for others than for ourselves.

For when is it that the desire is strongest in our hearts? When is it most apt to become invincible and inextinguishable? It is by the graveside of one whom we have loved. Such an one was brave and vigorous but a few hours ago. Now he is cold. There is a feeling in our hearts that a wrong has been done him whom we loved, if his activity, so bright and beautiful as it was, has been cut short. Our hearts revolt at the idea that the change which an hour has wrought in him is final and eternal.

Against this idea such poems as *Lycidas* or *Adonais* or *In Memoriam* are burning protests. They express not what we wish, but what we feel to be the due of the dead. We desire Immortality because without it the fate of others, even more than our own, leaves a feeling of dissatisfaction in our minds, as if a plan of which we had been permitted to see the outlines should lack completion for ever.

But is the desire more than a breathing of despair? Let us look at it more closely.

The desire for Immortality is the desire that the nature of Man may receive its legitimate consummation. It issues then from a study of human nature. As the process of the world tends to the supremacy of Man among the animals, so it tends to the supremacy of the psychical or spiritual part of human nature.

But the soul or spirit is seen to be progressing towards a certain goal. It is seen to be triumphing over its limitations and imperfections. It is seen to be approximating to the Divine. In the highest and holiest natures it is unmistakably tending towards a greater than human perfection. All at once, upon the theory of annihilation, the process ceases. This is the paradox from which human nature recoils. "We desire Immortality," says Jean Paul Richter, "not as the reward of virtue, but as its continuance." It is not the thought that *our* life or *our* virtue—it is the thought that virtue itself should die—which is soul-saddening. The desire for Immortality is like the desire in Man for happiness. Man desires happiness, he is capable of happiness, without happiness his life is incomplete and inharmonious. This is an argument that the Creator intended him to be happy. Similarly the thought or desire of Immortality is an argument that Man is an immortal being. For Immortality is essential to the purpose of human life; and if it is permissible to believe that life must fulfil its purpose, then it is necessary to believe in its Immortality. Thus Addison in his *Cato* has these lines :

> "It must be so ; Plato, thou reasonest well !
> Else whence this pleasing hope, this fond desire,
> This longing after Immortality ?
> Or whence this secret dread and inward horror
> Of falling into naught ? Why shrinks the soul
> Back on herself and startles at destruction ?
> 'Tis the Divinity that stirs within us ;
> 'Tis Heaven itself that points out an hereafter,
> And intimates eternity to Man." [1]

No doubt it may be said that this argument from the desire to the fact of Immortality depends upon

[1] Act v. scene 1.

the belief in the beneficence of the Almighty. It does so depend, but not entirely; for human nature is a witness to its own capacity, and there is that in Man which claims an immortal destiny. And this claim is not local or partial, but is found everywhere among all races and at all periods of History.

The desire of Immortality, like the religious sense (of which indeed it is a part), possesses the character of a universal creed. Everywhere Man is found to believe in God or in Divine or supernatural beings. Everywhere too he believes in the existence of souls or spirits after death.

It is true, indeed, that the universality of religion, as an element in human thought, has been denied. There is nothing perhaps that may not be denied. And even if primitive Man were not a religious being, it would be no disproof of religion. For upon speculative matters, as has been already said, it is not in the crude imaginations of savages but in the tendencies and judgments of civilised mankind that the truth may be more probably thought to reside. But modern anthropological research, by its patience and industry, has gone far to reassert the universality of the religious sentiment. Professor Max Müller puts it in these words, "We may safely say that, in spite of all researches, no human beings have been found anywhere who do not possess something which to them is religion, or to put it in the most general form, a belief in something beyond what they can see with their eyes." And he quotes from Professor Tiele this striking passage : "The statement that there are nations or tribes which possess no religion rests either on inaccurate observations or on a confusion of ideas. No tribe or nation has yet been met with destitute of belief in any higher beings, and travellers who asserted their existence have been afterwards refuted by facts. It is legitimate, therefore, to call religion in its most general sense an universal phenomenon of humanity." [1]

As it is with religion, so is it with the belief in the world beyond the grave. "The belief of mankind," says Mr. Alger, "that a soul or spirit survives the body has been so nearly universal as to appear like the spontaneous result of an instinct." [2]

It is true that the belief in the survival of the soul after death, like religion itself, was at first rudimentary; it was but the germ or promise of something

[1] *Hibbert Lectures*, ii. p. 79.
[2] *A Critical History of the Doctrine of the Future Life*, p. 583.

higher; it was sometimes so vague or faint that even keen observers could not detect it, but it was there; and whatever sanction a creed may claim, as having been widely and universally accepted at all stages of history, belongs to the faith that the soul of Man survives the grave. There is no people which does not exhibit that faith.

To the witness, then, of the soul's desire for Immortality (however that witness may be estimated) must be added the corroborating assurance of its universality.

Even this force it would be wrong to overestimate. I am contending for the reasonableness —the probability of faith in Immortality, not for its certainty. But one who recognises that the same, or the same sort of evidence, is adducible from history for the belief in Immortality as for religion itself, and that the one as well as the other is apparently a spontaneous universal outcome of the nature of Man, will probably feel himself strengthened in his conviction of a life surpassing and transcending the life of earth.

We may now summarise the evidences for

Immortality deducible from the nature of Man himself.

We have seen that Man is the climax of the visible creation; to him, as it were, the visible creation tends.

We have seen that in Man the spiritual part of his being is the highest, the most sacred, the nearest to God.

We have seen that according to analogy the separation of the soul from the body and the dissolution of the body does not necessitate or imply the death of the spirit.

We have seen that Man himself expects and demands Immortality; it is his hope, his guide, the postulate of his nature.

We have seen that this hope is strongest and most imperious in the highest and most God-like human natures.

We have seen intimations of an essential affinity between the highest part of human nature and the spiritual world.

We have seen that without human Immortality the great cosmical process is bereft of its full significance.

And we have seen that the conviction of personal

Immortality or survival after death has been at one period or other the universally prevalent faith of all races and all regions of mankind.

But these considerations, strong as they are, deserve to be weighed in the light of the Divine Nature (so far as it is known to us), and of that Nature viewed relatively to mankind.

In regard, then, to Immortality we will now consider the—

III. Evidence from the Being of God.

It has been no part of this essay to argue for the belief in God.

But it is obvious that that belief affects all other beliefs and aspects of belief. To one who holds the Being of God all Nature is full of hints, suggestions, and intimations which otherwise do not occur to the mind. Indeed, it is strange that men should make so much of differences among believers in God, however serious these differences may be, when the vital difference is between those whose view of nature is secular and materialistic, and those whose view is spiritual.

But if there is any belief which is sanctioned and enforced by faith in God, it is the belief in Immortality.

The two beliefs, in God and in Immortality, are complementary; they are linked together so indissolubly that, where the one is found, the other is sure to follow. As a rule, he who believes in God believes in Immortality, and he who believes in Immortality believes in God.

Thus Paley writes in his *Natural Theology:*

"It is one thing to maintain the doctrine of Providence along with that of a future state and another thing without it. In my opinion the two doctrines must stand or fall together. For although more of this apparent chance may perhaps upon other principles be accounted for than is generally supposed, yet a future state alone rectifies all disorders." [1]

To the Theist, then, the doctrine of Immortality is of as much concern as to the Christian. Without it Theism can no more than Christianity essay to solve the enigma of human life. And yet it is a doctrine appealing with special emphasis to Christian hearts. If it be true, as has been well said, that "all questions concerning human Immortality may be traced back to our idea of God," then it may be urged, as by Bishop Martensen, that "the God of

[1] Chap. xxvi.

Revelation is Love, and He therefore has interest in the monadic, the minute, and individual. He can find no adequate form of Revelation for Himself, save in a Kingdom of individuals who are immortal, and whom He will make partakers of His own eternity and blessedness. This is the proof of Immortality which Christ gives to the Sadducees when He says, 'God is not the God of the dead but of the living, for all live unto Him.'"[1]

The belief in God is encompassed with its own proper difficulties. But wherever the belief in God is found, there is found the belief in Immortality. The two are inseparable. For the face of the world is so hard to reconcile with a belief in the omnipotence and beneficence of the Creator that, if that belief exists, it cannot but postulate, as a corollary, the belief in a compensatory future.

In the last chapter, where the value of the belief in Immortality was set forth, certain considerations were urged; and it is these considerations and others like them which arise upon the theory of a Divine Almighty Providence. Thus it may be assumed that the purpose of God in Creation will

[1] *Christian Dogmatics*, § 274.

be ultimately achieved. Nature exhibits signs of purpose, it is clearly progressive; it is not drifting idly; it is making for an end. Nay, not so only, but the end of Nature is plainly associated with the destiny of Man. Whatever be the final goal of Nature, Man is involved in it. Of all created beings then Man is the last who, upon the hypothesis of a Providence, can be condemned to a hopeless and purposeless existence. Yet so it would be, if his life should end in death. Goethe seems to have felt this difficulty so keenly that it led him to his faith in Immortality. " Ich zweifle nicht an unserem Fortdauer, denn die Natur kann die Entelechie nicht entbehren."[1]

Human life indeed, in the point of view of religion, is a discipline. It is an education. But education points to something beyond itself. It is not understood unless in reference to futurity. Man is a scholar in the school of Divine Providence. He learns his lesson slowly and often painfully. If death is his end then, he dies before the lesson is learnt. This was the ground upon which Kant, in the name of the Practical Reason, postulated an end-

[1] "I have no doubt as to our continued existence, for Nature cannot forego her actuality (Entelechie)."—*Gespräche mit Eckermann*, vol. ii. p. 101.

less duration of personality, arguing that the moral law demanded infinite progress in the rational being, and that infinite progress was impossible except in Immortality.

The honour of God, it may almost be said without irreverence, is concerned in the satisfaction of the human desire for Immortality. For who can bear to think of the Creator as inspiring in human hearts a passionate and righteous sentiment, and making that sentiment the means by which Humanity is drawn into stronger sympathy and more loving intimacy with Himself, and then letting the sentiment fail of satisfaction at the last? But it is needless to press this point; for religious minds, impressed as they have been by the disciplinary character of life, have never failed to look beyond it to an Immortality.

Yet again the belief in the Eternity of God demands Immortality for those great attributes or ideas which centre in His Being. Such are the ideas of Truth, Justice, Purity, Love. We cannot conceive of these ideas as temporary or mutable. We are sure that they are immortal. If they are not endowed with Immortality, if they are not the same here and everywhere, now and for ever, then their claim upon the allegiance of Humanity disappears. So the poet sings :—

" Truth for truth and good for good ! The Good, the True, the Pure, the Just.
Take the charm 'For ever' from them, and they crumble into dust." [1]

But these ideas, as humanly conceived, are resident in the spirit. They are not of the body or the mind, but of the spirit. And if so, then the eternity of the ideas implies the eternity of the spirit which contains them.

It is needless to dwell upon the vindication of the Divine Equity and the Divine Providence within the spaces of the infinite future ; for this has been already considered as part of the satisfaction for which the human soul is permitted to look in Eternity. It is enough to say that the Almighty in virtue of His Infinity demands infinity wherein to reveal Himself to His creatures.

Let us, then, see what it is that the argument for Immortality from the Being of God may be said to amount to.

God is *ex hypothesi* perfect in Wisdom, in Power and in Love.

[1] Tennyson, *Locksley Hall, Sixty Years After.*

It is a justifiable expectation that He shall reveal the perfectness of His attributes to His sentient, intelligent and moral creatures. But the justification is not complete in the present life. It demands a life transcending and surviving the present.

Again, the Infinity of the Divine Nature characterises the moral qualities which are the necessary attributes of Divinity. But these qualities inform Humanity and invest it with an eternal character.

And, lastly, the disciplinary or educational character of the present life postulates a future life as a part of the Divine Counsel; and the spiritual or immortal element in Man, whereby he is allied to God, postulates Eternity.

This chapter, then, has suggested the external evidences for the soul's Immortality, *i.e.*, such evidences as lie in the constitution of the Universe, in the nature of Man, and in the Being of God.

It is now time to consider the internal evidences, *i.e.*, the witness of the soul to itself.

CHAPTER V

EVIDENCES FOR THE BELIEF

B. *Internal Evidences*

It has already been remarked that there is a difficulty in distinguishing the various evidences or lines of evidence for the great belief which is under consideration.

Even between the external and internal evidences (as they have been called) for the belief, it is not an easy thing to draw an absolute line.

Thus the Being of God is an external evidence for Immortality; but if Man be made, as he is, in the image of God, the eternity of God stands in direct relation to the eternity of Man.

Further the testimony of the soul to itself is an intricate question. We are concerned to know what is the nature of the soul. In the default or deficiency of external evidence we seek to learn from the soul itself what it is. But in so doing we are treating the subject of our inquiry as our witness.

Yet however difficult it may be to judge of the soul by studying the soul itself, no study can be more interesting, or so far as it can be prosecuted, more convincing. To some minds it will seem the only satisfactory way of arriving at a conclusion respecting the probable destiny of the soul.

Thus Emerson says, "Immortality is a doctrine too great to rest on any legend, that is on any man's experience but our own. It must be proved, if at all, from our own activity and designs which imply an interminable future for their play."[1]

Such a statement clearly means that the study of the soul in itself will produce a conviction of its Immortality.

What, then, is the soul?

The soul in its proper nature has been the subject of discussion and, so far as possible, of definition in the first chapter. It has been defined as the total sum of the intellectual, moral and spiritual faculties belonging to human nature. In Dr. Martineau's explicit words already quoted it is "the

[1] *Conduct of Life.* Essay on *Worship.*

constant centre to which we refer all our acts as their source and all our experiences as their receptacle."

It is not now with the soul, abstractedly considered, but with its faculties or qualities as leading to a belief in its immortal destiny, that we are concerned. And of these there are four which have been recognised, more or less widely, by philosophical thinkers, in modern times and in ancient, as attributes characteristic of Immortality, viz., its immateriality, its indissolubility, its spontaneous energy, and its affinity to the Divine Nature. Each of these four qualities has, at some time or other, been held to be in itself a sufficient proof that the soul is immortal; but the cumulative evidence of all is necessarily more forcible than the evidence of any one taken by itself. It will be well to consider them in order, and first—

(1) The *immateriality* of the soul.

It must be admitted that this argument will not appeal to one who takes a material, and not a spiritual, view of the Universe. If there is nothing in the Universe but what is material, then either there is no such thing as soul, or the soul is material and therefore mortal. The belief in the immateriality of the soul is a spiritual belief and, as being such, it coincides with the belief in God. But this is only one more proof that speculation concerning the nature or destiny of the soul must go back ultimately to the question of the Divine Being. To hold that there is no such thing as soul or spirit is to hold that there is no God; for God is Spirit, and the spiritual world is, so to say, the reflexion of His Eternal Spiritual Presence.

It has been urged in the last chapter that the faiths in God and in an Immortal Life are correlative; each of them, not only in fact but in logic, implies the other.

In arguing, then, from the immateriality of the soul to its Immortality, it is necessary to assume the existence of spirit and a spiritual world. But if that assumption is once made, there can be no doubt that the soul is not material but spiritual. But matter is perishable, or more strictly, dissoluble. The soul, then, being immaterial is imperishable, or to put the argument in a syllogistic form :

It is a property of matter to perish or to be dissolved ;

But the soul is immaterial ;

Therefore the soul is imperishable ; or to speak

correctly, the perishableness of matter affords no presumption that the soul will perish.

The argument so stated must not be pressed unduly. It is in effect rather negative than positive. It does not prove the Immortality of the soul, but it proves that the Immortality is possible. For as the signs and evidences of dissolution are all associated with matter, it follows that they do not and cannot apply to any immaterial or spiritual entity. The utmost which it is possible to say is that the laws of the material world are more or less known, the laws of the spiritual world are unknown; but, inasmuch as spirit is wholly different from matter, it is reasonable to conceive of the spiritual laws as different from the material.

Still the fact of the soul's immateriality, as tending to establish its immortal destiny, has so greatly influenced Christian thought, and indeed amounts to so high an evidential probability, that it demands a sympathetic regard.

To quote one authority out of many:

Thomas Aquinas argues that the soul, like God Himself, like the angels, is a *forma separata*, *i.e.*, an immaterial form; and that, as being immaterial, it is immortal, as such a form cannot in the nature of things destroy itself, nor can it by the dissolution of any material underlying substance be destroyed.[1]

The Schoolmen generally under the influence of Aquinas rested their belief in the soul's Immortality not indeed wholly, but in a large degree upon its immaterial nature. And from them the belief in the soul's immateriality as a positive doctrine has descended to modern thought, and, wherever the distinction between soul and matter has been realised, the Immortality of the soul has been held to be a natural consequence of its immateriality.

(2) But when it has been asked why the immateriality of the soul constitutes deathlessness, then has emerged the second of the arguments adduced on internal grounds for Immortality, viz., that the soul is in its nature indissoluble, and that *indissolubility* precludes destruction or death.

This is perhaps a philosophical rather than a religious argument. It finds its first and simplest expression in the *Phædo*.[2] Socrates there argues that "the soul is in the very likeness of the Divine and immortal and intellectual and uniform and indissoluble and unchangeable; and that the body

---

[1] *Summa Theologiæ*, part i., question lxxv.
[2] *Phædo*, p. 80.

is in the very likeness of the human and mortal and unintellectual and multiform and dissoluble and changeable," and that, as the body itself is not at once dissolved by death, but remains intact for a time, and if it be embalmed in the Egyptian manner, for an indefinitely long time, it is impossible to conceive of the soul as being destroyed as soon as it has left the body; the soul will rather depart in peace to the invisible world which is its true home.

As often happens, the proof which Socrates gives of his tenet is rather suggested than expressed; but it lies, as may be seen, in the assumed affinity of the nature of the soul to the Divine Nature.

However, the view that the soul is indissoluble and therefore immortal has been widely entertained in Christian Theology.

Thus Gregory of Nyssa, after speaking of the "vivifying influence of the soul as exercised in a mysterious manner upon the body, urges that as, while the framework of the body still holds together, each individual part is possessed of a soul which penetrates equally every component member . . . so, when that framework is dissolved, and has returned to its kindred elements, there is nothing against probability that that simple and incomposite essence (ἁπλῆ καὶ ἀσύνθετος φύσις) which has once for all by some inexplicable law grown with the growth of the bodily framework, should continually remain beside the atoms with which it has been blended, and should in no way be sundered from a union once formed. For it does not follow that, because the composite is dissolved, the incomposite must be dissolved with it."[1]

Somewhat similar is the argument of Augustine: "The nature of the soul itself has no kind of material existence in space. For whatever consists of any kind of gross matter must necessarily be divisible into parts, having one in one place and another in another. . . . The nature of the soul, on the other hand, though we leave out of account its power of perceiving truth, and consider only its inferior power of giving unity to the body, and of sensation in the body, does not appear to have any material extension in space. For it is all present in each separate part of its body when it is all present in any sensation. There is not a smaller part in the finger, and a larger in the arm, as the bulk of the finger is less than that of the arm; but the quantity

---

[1] *On the Soul and the Resurrection*, p. 437, in the Select Library of the Nicene and post-Nicene Fathers.

everywhere is the same; for the whole is present everywhere. For when the finger is touched, the whole mind feels, though the sensation is not through the whole body. No part of the mind is unconscious of the touch, which proves the presence of the whole." [1]

Or to come to modern theologians; Bishop Berkeley says:

"We have shown that the soul is indivisible, incorporeal, unextended, and it is consequently *incorruptible*. Nothing can be plainer than that the motions, changes, decays, and dissolutions which we hourly see befall natural bodies (and that is what we mean by the *course of nature*) cannot possibly affect an *active, simple, uncompounded* substance. Such a being, therefore, is indissoluble by the force of nature, that is to say, the *soul of man* is naturally *immortal*." [2]

And Bishop Butler:

"All presumption of death's being the destruction of living beings must go upon the supposition that they are compounded, and so discerptible. But since consciousness is a single and indivisible power, it should seem that the subject in which it

---

[1] *Against the Epistle of Manichæus*, chap. xvi., also in the Select Library of the Nicene and post-Nicene Fathers.
[2] *The Principles of Human Knowledge*, part i. § 141.

resides must be so too.... It has been argued and, for anything appearing to the contrary, justly, that since the perception or consciousness which we have of our own existence is indivisible, so that it is a contradiction to suppose one part of it should be here and the other there; the perceptive power, or the power of consciousness, is indivisible too, and consequently the subject in which it resides, *i.e.*, the conscious being." [1]

But these opinions of philosophical theologians demand corroboration from other masters of philosophical thought.

The following is the language of Descartes :—

"Je remarque ici qu'il y a une grande différence entre l'esprit et le corps, en ce que le corps, de sa nature, est toujours divisible, et que l'esprit est entièrement indivisible ; car en effet, quand je le considère, c'est-à-dire, quand je me considère moi-même en tant que je suis seulement une chose qui pense, je ne puis distinguer en moi aucunes parties, mais je connais et conçois fort clairement que je suis une chose absolument une et entière." [2]

It was this view of the soul's simplicity or indi-

---

[1] *Analogy*, part i., chap. i.
[2] *Discours de la Méthode. Méditation sixième.*

visibility which led Descartes to place it locally in the *glans pinealis*.

Leibnitz was naturally disposed by his monadic theory to believe in the indissolubility and the indestructibility of the soul. He says of it : " Tout esprit étant comme un monde à part suffisant à lui-même, indépendant de toute autre créature, enveloppant l'infini, exprimant l'univers, est aussi durable, aussi subsistant et aussi absolu que l'univers même des créatures."[1]

Modern philosophers have been comparatively little occupied with the structural or formative nature of the soul. The idea of the soul, like that of Heaven itself, has passed imperceptibly by common consent into the region of the immaterial. And, at least since Kant's influence became predominant, there has, I think, been no one who has sought to define the nature of the soul, and has conceived of it otherwise than as a simple indivisible or spiritual entity and, in virtue of being so, immortal.

But the precise nature of the argument from the immateriality of the soul to its Immortality remains to be stated.

[1] *Système nouveau de la Nature, p.* 128.

What is the *differentia* or distinctive character of the soul ?

It seems to be this :—

The soul may be conceived as consisting of parts, like the body. It is possible and natural to speak of the intellectual, the moral, the spiritual parts, *i.e.*, faculties, of the soul, as of the brain, heart, arms, legs, &c., of the body. But in the soul the distinction (so far as can be observed) is speculative only; in the body it is actual.

Thus a part of the body can be cut off; it becomes then a separate material substance. But no mutilation of the soul is possible or conceivable.

Again, the body is visibly subject to dissolution at death. But there is no such evidence of the soul's dissolution.

The soul is, as it were, a unit or atom; but an atom is indissoluble and indestructible; the soul therefore must be conceived as enduring eternally.

If it be asked, What is the logical value of this argument? the answer seems to be that the atomic nature of the soul, *i.e.*, its indivisibility, is philosophically a more tenable view than the opposite; and it constitutes an *a priori* probability of the soul's Immortal Life; but the indissolubility, as well as the immateriality, of the soul is but preparatory as an evidence for the phenomena which support with greater impressiveness the doctrine of Immortality.

(3) It has often been thought that the intrinsic *energy* or activity of the soul is an indication of its character, and so of its destiny.

The soul, it has been said, is the source of movement; it acts, it is not primarily acted upon; and, as being itself the source of movement, it cannot become motionless, *i.e.*, dead. Upon this view the soul is in a measure fettered and cramped by the body in life, but death sets it free, and it enters then upon a larger life. By nobody has this view been expressed or advocated in clearer language than by Plato in the *Phædrus*.

"The soul" (says Socrates) "through all her being is immortal, for that which is ever in motion is immortal; but that which moves another and is moved by another, in ceasing to move, ceases also to live. Only the self-moving, never leaving self, never ceases to move, and is the fountain and beginning of motion to all that moves besides. Now the beginning is unbegotten, for that which is begotten has a beginning; but the beginning is begotten of nothing, for if it were begotten of something, then the begotten would not come from a beginning. But if unbegotten, it must be also indestructible; for if beginning were destroyed, there could be no beginning out of anything, nor anything out of a beginning; and all things must have a beginning. And therefore the self-moving is the beginning of motion, and this can neither be destroyed nor begotten; else the whole heavens and all creation would collapse and stand still, and never again have motion or birth. But if the self-moving is proved to be immortal, he who affirms that self-motion is the very idea and essence of the soul will not be put to confusion. For the body which is moved from without is soulless; but that which is moved from within has a soul, for such is the nature of the soul. But if this be true, must not the soul be self-moving, and therefore of necessity unbegotten and immortal?"[1]

Nor is this an ancient philosophic fancy which has exercised no influence upon thought in Christian and modern times. No doubt it is true that Plato did not distinguish so carefully as later thinkers between the Soul or informing principle of the Universe and individual souls. It has sometimes seemed to me that the world-soul (if I may call it so)

[1] p. 245, C-E. Cp. *Laws*, p. 896 A, B.

of Plato stood in his philosophy in a parallel relation, though vastly inferior, to that of the Holy Spirit of God in Christian Theology to the spirit of each individual man. But the inference of the soul's Immortality from its absolute intrinsic energy has commended itself in one way or another to numerous and different minds, as *e.g.*, to Athanasius when he wrote in his treatise *contra Gentes*,[1] " If, as we have shown, the soul moves the body and is not moved by other things, it follows that the movement of the soul is spontaneous, and that this spontaneous movement goes on after the body is laid aside in the earth. . . If the soul is moved by itself, it follows that it outlives the body"; or to Goethe, when he said in conversation with Eckerman, "The conviction of our continued existence arises in my mind from the conception of activity. For if I work unceasingly until my end, Nature is bound to allot me another form of existence, as the present form can no longer support my spirit "[2]; or to Byron, who wrote in his diary, "Of the immortality of the soul it appears to me that there can be but little doubt, if we attend for a moment to the action of mind. It is in perpetual activity."

[1] Chap. 33. [2] *Gespräche mit Goethe*, vol. ii. p. 40.

It is difficult to resist the force of this argument. The body and the soul, as constituents of human nature, stand in sharp contrast. The body in itself is mere brute matter, dull, motionless, inert. It is so apart from the soul. It is so when the soul leaves it at death. But the body when tenanted by the soul is alive and mobile ; it is impelled and directed by the energy of the soul. And this motive power the soul possesses in itself. But if the motive power is inherent in the soul, it is eternal, it is as perpetual as it is spontaneous, and we cannot conceive of it as ceasing to be. Therefore, as the motion is eternal, the soul which is its centre and source is eternal also.

Consciousness reveals too that the soul is not only the motive power of the body, but that in its own movements it is independent wholly or mainly of the body. Thus, while the body remains stationary, the soul, *i.e.*, the mind, ranges at will over time and space ; it can be a thousand miles from the body, while still associated with it ; it can conjure up the distant past or remote localities ; it is uncontrolled and uncontrollable ; it treats the body more as a slave than as a master.

It is true that this argument is in a sense logically

allied to the case for the freedom of the will. For if there be an original spontaneity of the soul, then is it free, and that which is free is immortal. But whether this freedom be admitted or not, it is clear that, if the soul survives death, it emerges after death into a larger life. For upon any reasonable estimate of the contrast or antagonism between the soul and the body it can hardly be doubtful that the influence of the body upon the soul is limiting and darkening; it cramps and thwarts the soul and prevents it from enjoying the full light and the complete liberty for which it yearns. This is an experience that deserves to be regarded as universal; for there is no man who is not, in his personal struggle with evil, conscious of the inimical and perilous energy of "the flesh."

The soul, then, so long as it is imprisoned in the body, is like a captive, conscious of powers which cannot be fully or properly exercised under the conditions of the terrestrial life. But it follows, as a natural inference, that the soul, when it is emancipated from its present limiting conditions, will or may assert the fulness of these powers in the serene and holy atmosphere of Heaven.

(4) And this anticipation of the soul's future leads to the last attribute which has been felt

by many thinkers as constituting a witness of the soul to its own Immortality, viz., its *Divinity*, or, to speak more strictly, its affinity to the Divine Nature.

For if it is an indication, as it has appeared to be, of Immortality, that the soul should possess an intrinsic and unfailing energy, the indication is greatly corroborated when that energy is found to place the soul in direct and intimate relation to God. An energy which is elevating, spiritualising and sanctifying is a witness that is so strong as to be conclusive. Let us look, then, at the vaticinations of the soul respecting itself.

The soul's conception of its own Immortality has often been held to prove that it is essentially immortal. Man, it has been said, cannot logically think of himself as dead. It is necessary to him to conceive of himself as living. But Man may be what he can imagine himself to be. The inability, then, to realise personal annihilation is a just evidence that personality will endure.

Again, the native gifts or qualities of the soul are such as bear the imprint or presage of infinity. They admit of no satisfaction in a limited present; they augur a limitless futurity. Thought, hope, love, faith, devotion are in their nature infinite, and, as such, they postulate an infinite future. No human being can be said to exhaust the capacities of these qualities upon earth. However great his satisfactions and enjoyments may be, they leave always a void, a yearning consciousness of something better and more enduring than the present. And capacities which are infinite expect Immortality. "There are wondrous impulses in us," it has been said, "constitutional convictions prescient of futurity, like those prevising instincts in birds leading them to take preparatory flights before their actual migration."[1]

Such are the intimations of Immortality within the soul. They are the witnesses to the soul's true character. For that which is capable of immortal thought is capable of Immortality. The soul moves, as it were, in a larger than earthly atmosphere. It deals with infinite space, infinite time, infinite aspiration. But infinity is a conception that transcends experience. The conception of infinity, therefore, proves Immortality.

The study of the human soul reveals it as ever reaching out beyond and above itself to a super-

---

[1] Alger, *A Critical History of the Doctrine of the Future Life*, p. 50.

natural attainment and advancement. Its capacities of knowledge, of virtue and of devotion remain on earth ever unsatisfied. Man is like a traveller in some mountainous country who has no sooner surmounted one lofty ridge than he sees another, still more arduous, rising before him. He never is or will be upon earth what he feels he might be, what he knows he ought to be. It is to this unsatisfied capacity of human nature that Addison alludes in a striking passage of the *Spectator*.[1] "Among other excellent arguments for the immortality of the soul, there is one drawn from the perpetual progress of the soul to its perfection, without a possibility of ever arriving at it. How can it enter into the thoughts of man that the soul which is capable of such immense perfections and of receiving new improvements to all eternity, shall fall away into nothing almost as soon as it is created? ... To look upon the soul as going on from strength to strength, to consider that she is to shine for ever with new accessions of glory and brighten to all eternity, that she will be still adding virtue to virtue and knowledge to knowledge, carries in it some-

[1] *Spectator*, No. iii.

thing wonderfully agreeable to that ambition which is natural to the mind of Man." Or, as a modern writer says, "We believe Man immortal, not because, as is pretended, thought and consciousness cannot be annihilated; but because the human intellectual and moral structure is such as to imply an after stage of expansion."[1]

But we have not yet reached the supreme point of this argument.

It is not in the intellectual or emotional part of human nature that Man's affinity to God is most clearly seen.

Man consists, it has been said, of body, soul and spirit.

The Divine part of his nature is the spirit.

In his body he is as the brutes.

In his soul, *i.e.*, in his reason and emotion, he is raised above the brutes, but not entirely removed from them.

In his spirit he is as the angels in Heaven.

The spirit of Man is the faculty wherein reside his faith, his reverence, his passionate desire for God.

Why should it be thought a thing incredible that Man should enter into communion with his

[1] Isaac Taylor, *Physical Theory of Another Life*, p. 233.

Maker? Why should the spiritual experiences of the saints—of a St. Francis or a St. Teresa—their intuitions of Divine truth, their visions of Heaven, their raptures and solaces and revelations — why should they all be brushed aside by rude secular hands, as though they were unworthy of a serious regard? When full allowance is made for the possibilities of self-deception, which is as much a peril of the senses as of the spirit, it is, I think, impossible to doubt the reality of the communion that holy men and women in all Christian ages have held with the Father of Spirits. Nay, it is not to the saints only as the prize of victory, but to all true humble souls which are striving after God, that there come ever and again high rapturous moments when earthly passions and ambitions fall away and the secret of life—the purport of being—stands revealed. To this ever-accumulating body of evidence religion appeals. It is the heritage of faith. It is not of one place or time, but universal. It is the eternal witness of the human spirit to its Divine Original, to the Home from which it came and to which it returns. "The Spirit itself beareth witness with our spirit, that we are the children of God."

When it is said in Holy Scripture that Man is made in the image of his Maker, it is his spirit which is the main (though not, I think, the only) point of resemblance. "Patet dei effigies," as Calvin says, "ad totam præstantiam qua eminet hominis natura inter omnes animantium species."[1] But the spirit is the pre-eminent faculty; it is a part of the Divine Nature in Man.

The poets and philosophers of antiquity were not unconscious of an affinity between the Divine and human natures. St. Paul, addressing the Athenians, could quote from "certain of their own poets" the words, "we are also His offspring." But it was Christianity that evinced the reality and dignity of this Divine sonship. The Incarnation of the Son of God created the persuasion that all men, as He deigned to call them His "brethren," were children of His Father.

If it may be concluded, then, that the spiritual faculty in Man is the witness, as it is the centre, of his affinity to the Godhead, how great is the duty of cultivating the spiritual life! I know no

---

[1] "The image of God extends to the whole excellency by which Man's nature surpasses all the species of living things."—*Institutes*, i. xv. 3.

more striking passage even of Pauline theology than that in which St. Paul teaches that "the natural (ψυχικὸς) man receiveth not the things of the Spirit of God, for they are foolishness unto him; neither knoweth he them, because they are spiritually discerned;" and again, "God hath revealed them unto us by His Spirit; for the Spirit searcheth all things, yea, the deep things of God."[1]

The spirit of Man, like the body or the mind, has its own laws of development or decay. In one man the voice of the Spirit is dominant and authoritative; in another it speaks but in a whisper. The spiritual or eternal verities which are in one life the strongest and surest of all motives to conduct are in another perhaps uncertain, vague and nebulous. And the inference is that he who would attain to spiritual knowledge must educate and elevate his spirit by the processes which the spiritual experience of mankind justifies and recommends as the conditions of the spiritual life. He must become a spiritual man.

[1] 1 Cor. ii. The adjective ψυχικός must clearly be interpreted here in the lower or narrower of its two meanings; it excludes the spirit (πνεῦμα).

We may now summarise the conclusions of this chapter.

The soul, or, in exact Theology, the spirit, is the highest element in human nature. It is immaterial and indissoluble; it is therefore immortal.

In its intellectual, and yet more in its moral and spiritual prerogatives, it is allied to the Divine Nature; it may therefore be reasonably held to participate in the Divine attribute of Immortality.

By its capacity for infinite thought and infinite desire it expects infinity.

It possesses in itself the spring of action; but that which is self-moved is imperishable.

And finally the cultivation of the spiritual life exalts human nature to the region of the Divine. For the spirit of Man is akin to the Divine Spirit.

And here this chapter might close but that it is natural to examine how far the considerations adduced as evidences, whether external or internal, for Immortality are found to harmonise in respect of the lower animals, with the probability of their fate if estimated, as in the last chapter, by a general reference to the constitution of the Universe.

For it is always possible to take the case for

human Immortality and determine how far it is or is not applicable to the lower animals. Now, while the law of conservation is an argument suitable to the lower animals, it is evident that no such argument can be derived from the dignity or progressiveness of their nature. Similarly the souls of animals are immaterial and indissoluble, as well as human souls; they are gifted, though in a limited degree, with native energy; but they possess and exhibit no affinity to the Godhead. The probable inference would seem to be that animals are immortal, but not immortal in the same sense as men. Some characteristics of Immortality their life exhibits, but not all. Nor can it be urged that God may be reasonably expected to justify His Providence to them as to mankind; for there is no sign that they feel the intellectual and moral difficulties which have so grievously embarrassed Humanity. A probable but limited Immortality, *i.e.*, limited in the capacity for knowledge and reverence, is at the most all that awaits them, if it be judged by philosophical speculation.

But when the thought proceeds to Christ's revelation and to His express teaching, especially that not one sparrow falls to earth without His Father, and then to St. Paul's great anticipation of a future in which the whole creation, not Humanity alone, now "made subject to vanity," shall be enriched with a glorious and sacred liberty, it is an immediate inference that the Eternal Mercy has reserved some beneficent destiny for the animals. For they too suffer in the present life as well as men, nay, they suffer for the follies and cruelties of mankind; and the principle of Divine compensation suggests, if it does not compel, a belief in regeneration for them.

Thus the conclusion to which the study of the soul in itself leads in respect of the lower animals harmonises with the inference already drawn from the constitution of the Universe. It establishes a probability that they are immortal, although not immortal in the same sense as Man. Beyond this probability it is difficult or impossible to go.

But there still remains two points regarding human Immortality.

It was an old question among the Christian Fathers whether the Immortality of the soul ($\psi v \chi \acute{\eta}$) was a quality natural and native to it, or an acquisition, being something imparted to it in virtue of its union with the spirit ($\pi v \epsilon \hat{v} \mu a$) at Baptism or in any other way. The question may not be thought important, nor does it affect the considerations which have been urged in this essay as justifying or encouraging a belief in Immortality. Still it was the subject of differing opinions at various epochs of Church History. Thus on the one side as advocates of the soul's natural Immortality are Tertullian and Origen, as advocates of imparted Immortality Justin Martyr (though his expressions are not wholly clear), Tatian, and Irenæus; on the one side Augustine and Gregory the Great, on the other Lactantius; on the one side Thomas Aquinas, on the other Duns Scotus. The defences and indeed the expositions of their opinions lie beyond the proper scope of this essay. But upon the whole the weight of authority inclined at all times to the doctrine of the natural Immortality of the soul. At last in 1513 A.D. the Lateran Council declared the natural Immortality of the soul to be an article of the Faith. Faustus Socinus indeed argued that the soul was naturally mortal, and so at a later time did Dodswell (though less explicitly) in his controversy with Clarke. But in the Catholic Church the doctrine of the soul's absolute, intrinsic, natural Immortality has long remained unshaken. It is, as was said in the first chapter, the belief that is advocated in this essay, not so much upon distinctively Christian as upon general religious and philosophical grounds. For any supposition that the soul can or may perish necessarily impairs the validity of all such arguments as may be urged, in favour of its immortal destiny, from the nature of the soul itself. The soul is its own witness; it reveals its own Immortality.

That it is difficult to define physiologically the character of the union between soul and body, or the precise manner or time in which that union is effected, must be admitted by all candid thinkers. But the beginnings of things are always difficult; and it is no less difficult to conceive how life originated in the humblest of animate beings than how the soul, with its vast intellectual and spiritual capacities, entered into union with the body of Man.

The absolute intrinsic Immortality of every soul is the Catholic doctrine, and it is for that that this essay contends.

The second question is the following:

It is said that the arguments for the soul's Immortality, in so far as they support its continued existence after death, equally support its pre-existence before its association with the body.

Upon this point a difference would seem to exist between ancient and modern philosophical thought.

The ancient writers who believed in the soul's Immortality generally believed not only that it would exist after death but that it had existed before birth. The argument of the *Phædo*, for instance, especially that part of it which turns upon the soul's reminiscence of knowledge acquired in a previous state, tends to prove the pre-existence rather than the post-existence of the soul. Nor was this theory of the soul's life absent from Jewish Theology; for it is implied in such a passage as that of the Wisdom of Solomon, " Being good I came into a body undefiled,"[1] and it is expressly taught in the Talmud. It descended to some Christian theologians, *e.g.*, to Origen. In recent poetry it is the central thought of Wordsworth's *Ode on the Intimations of Immortality*.

And whatever strength there is in the primitive creeds of mankind may be enlisted on behalf of

[1] viii. 20.

the soul's pre-existence; for travellers are practically unanimous in reporting that the belief in Immortality among savage races is everywhere a belief that the soul not only will survive death but existed before birth.

Among modern writers, influenced as they have been consciously or unconsciously by Christianity, it has been the custom to let the question of the soul's pre-existence drop out of sight. A few thinkers, as *e.g.*, Fichte, have raised it more or less sympathetically. But whether from a dread of any approach to the pagan theory of metempsychosis or from a sense that personal responsibility is bound up with the limitation of the soul's life to the present and the future, or from other causes, modern writers have in general confined themselves to arguing for survival after death, without much reference to the possible existence of the soul before its birth in the body.

Yet many considerations which make for the one belief make for the other. The fact of immateriality, the fact of inherent energy, the fact of Divine affinity would all suggest, if they do not imply, the absence of a creative point or moment in the history of the soul. Philosophically indeed it is less difficult to conceive of the soul as existing eternally than as coming into existence at a specified time for the sake of association with the body. And if the question of the soul's existence were purely philosophical, there would seem no doubt that a belief in the soul's eternity—viz. that, as it always will be, so it always was—recommends itself to the reason.

It is evident indeed, as Dr. Martineau has observed, that post-existence does not *prove* pre-existence. "Within the limits of organic life, whose history consists of a cycle of chemical changes, it is true that birth is the invariable precursor of a series leading to death; but beyond this range it cannot be shown that either mechanical or mental genesis must run its course and come to an end. What indeed does Newton's first law declare, but that a particle once set in motion in empty space will continue to move in a straight line with uniform velocity for ever unless some external force supervenes?"[1] But, apart from the creative Will of God, it remains probable that the soul, as possessing in itself the strength of Immortality, had no beginning, as it will have no end.

[1] *A Study of Religion*, book iv., chap. iv. vol. ii. p. 334.

Thus the argument, like all other arguments touching the soul, leads back to the Being of God.

The pre-existence of the soul must remain a surmise, a possibility, or at the most a probability.

Its immortal existence after death is a belief supported by so many strong evidential considerations, upon the hypothesis of a Divine Almighty Providence, that it merits to be held and followed as a belief and a motive in life.

Thus it is that the consideration of Immortality is felt to be none other than the consideration of God Himself. The belief in the Being of God and the belief in the immortal existence of the soul are intimately and inextricably united. God has joined them together; and Man may not put them asunder.

Upon the whole I see no convincing argument (in spite of much probability) for the soul's Immortality apart from the sublime belief in Him.

To my mind there are but two logical positions which the human reason can permanently assume towards the complex phenomena of life.

The one is sheer dark absolute Materialism.

The other is Theism with its inherent probability of such a communication from God to Man as is called Revelation, and its stronger, because more subjective, probability of a soul other than material transcending time and space and asserting its kinship with Heaven.

Between these beliefs the religious spirit will not long hesitate to choose.

CHAPTER VI

THE CHRISTIAN AMPLIFICATION OF THE BELIEF

THIS essay has hitherto been concerned with the general evidences for the Immortality of the soul. These are such evidences as are in the main independent of any special religious belief, although they presuppose a spiritual attitude of mind. No doubt it is true that the estimate formed of these evidences will be, or may be, influenced by a particular creed. Thus to a Christian the authority of Christ Himself is final; it cannot be resisted or disputed; and as soon as it becomes clear that He announced authoritatively this or that truth concerning Immortality, there can no more be any question about it.

But it would be wrong to connect the belief in Immortality, or to connect it exclusively, with any special form of creed. It is a belief natural to all persons who take a religious view of human nature. It is in fact the common property of all the great spiritual systems of belief in the world.

The belief in Immortality is a philosophical as well as a religious doctrine. It is chiefly upon philosophical grounds that the belief has been recommended in this essay. Yet no sooner is it accepted as a matter of Philosophy than it becomes stamped with a religious type or character. It is in fact what religion makes it to be. Thus a Mohammedan may believe in Immortality as well as a Christian ; but he does not believe in the same Immortality. Immortality is one thing, Christian Immortality is another.

And it is not the mere abstract doctrine but the *Christian* doctrine of Immortality which is the faith of Christian souls in a Christian land. This is, in effect, the doctrine advocated in this essay ; for it cannot be doubted that no system of Philosophy or Religion has done so much to invest the thought of the Immortal Life with a definite consistent character as Christianity. St. Paul in one of his Epistles, speaking of his Divine Master, says that He " only hath Immortality ;"[1] and in another that He

[1] 1 Timothy vi. 16.

"hath abolished death and hath brought life and immortality (or 'incorruption') to light through the Gospel."[1] Immortality, then, is the dominant note in the Christian Revelation. It pervades and influences Christ's whole teaching. And the Christian Revelation, above all other teachings, has not only impressed upon human minds and consciences the fact of personal Immortality, but has elucidated, or at least suggested, in various manners, what the nature of Immortality may be. It may be laid down, then, in Tennyson's words, that "the cardinal point of Christianity is the Life after Death."[2]

It is indeed the function of religious philosophy to create, by more or less persuasive arguments, a belief in Immortality; but it is the function of special revelations to fill up the space of the Immortal Life. The mere philosophical belief is as the outline of a picture; but it is from religion that the picture derives its form, colour, completeness, reality, truth. The Immortal Life, as regarded by minds of highest intellectuality and spirituality, is not mere existence; it is existence characterised and conditioned by the Revelation of Jesus Christ.

Christianity does not prove Immortality. It as-

---

[1] 2 Timothy i. 10.   [2] *Life of Tennyson*, vol. i. p. 321.

sumes Immortality; or to speak exactly, it breathes a spiritual atmosphere in which the assumption of Immortality is felt to be natural or even necessary. But taking Immortality as a fact, Christianity impresses upon it a character.

Is it possible to determine that character?

Immortality, as an abstract, colourless dogma, possesses no adequate satisfaction for mankind. It may be held to gratify the longing for continued life. But we desire to know not only that we shall live after death but, so far as possible, what our life will be, and where and under what conditions it will be, and how we may so acquit ourselves in the present as to attain the reward of felicity in the future. And to all such questions Jesus Christ affords an answer, not indeed as absolute or definite (at least apparently) as human curiosity is prone to demand, but sufficient for the conduct of life, for the inspiration of duty, and for the satisfaction of the "obstinate questionings" which are the witnesses of the affinity of human nature to the Divine.

We believe, then, not in Immortality alone, but in Christian Immortality. We are not philosophers only, or Theists; we are more than these, we are disciples of our Lord Jesus Christ.

It is important, therefore, to apprehend the special light of Christ's Revelation upon the nature of Immortality.

But His revelation of Immortality is only a part of His general Revelation. It must be interpreted in the same manner and spirit as any other truth revealed within the Gospels; that is to say, that the interpretation of it must pay due regard to the character of His teaching and of the record in which it is contained, as well as to His personal claim and authority in His human life.

Now Jesus Christ was Divine but also human, human but also Divine. The speculations of recent thought upon His Nature, however little they may be affected by Christian orthodoxy, tend convergingly to the belief that He was Man and yet superior to Man, or in the precise words of the Creed, that He was "equal to the Father as touching His Godhead, and inferior to the Father as touching His Manhood." No representation of His Person as solely Divine or as solely human has failed to end, soon or late, in contradiction or paradox. That it is difficult, if not impossible, to express the truth of His Nature in words must be admitted; it is part of the difficulty affecting the relation of Man to God in every aspect. But religious belief may transcend its verbal expression. For if logic is the one safe guide in human matters, it is not so in Divine. Where theological truth is unattainable or incommunicable, it is not always in a simple positive proposition, it is often in the balance of two parallel and apparently opposed propositions, as F. W. Robertson pointed out long ago, that the best approximation to the Divine reality seems to lie. Jesus Christ "emptied Himself" of His Glory. What was the absolute nature of that self-emptying or, as the theological term is, *Kenosis*, and in what form or degree it is a limitation of His Omniscience, is a question disputed among theologians; but the question does not fall within the scope of this essay. It is enough to bear in mind that His Godhead, during the period of His human life, was "veiled in flesh."

Jesus Christ lived on earth the common life of men. There was nothing that distinguished Him externally from His contemporaries. No fact is clearer in the Gospels than that men and women who knew Him, consorted with Him, listened to His teachings, and were the recipients of His charities, might remain unconscious, and as it seems, wholly unsuspicious of any characteristic Divine prerogative attaching to His Person. Apart from sin, and perhaps from sickness, which is the shadow of sin, He was subject to human infirmities. He was hungry and thirsty, and weary as at Jacob's well. He shed tears as He drew near to the grave of Lazarus. In Gethsemane He prayed that the cup of agony might be taken from Him, and it was not so taken ; He drank it to the dregs.

But the point is that His doctrine, like His life, though essentially Divine, was yet in a sense conditioned by His humanity. He used the current language of the world. It was indeed impossible that He should speak otherwise ; there is no celestial language upon earth. The verities of the spiritual Immortal Life are in themselves neither definable in human words nor intelligible to human apprehensions. Our Lord sought to recommend them to the souls and consciences of His hearers not in precise scientific phraseology, but far more impressively, by figure and parable and allegory. His language exhibits no attempt at representing Divine things as they are in themselves. He taught them in such a manner as the world was able to understand ; and the result has been that His teaching has dominated and determined the speculations of most religious thinkers upon the invisible world.

All or nearly all that He said about the future life is found to be figurative. Parables such as that of Dives and Lazarus, pictorial scenes such as that of the Advent of the Son of Man in His glory, are far removed from the accuracy of scientific literalism. They bring home great and general truths to the heart of the world ; but to press every detail, to insist upon every clause and word of them as literally exact, is to mistake the whole character of His teaching. It is difficult to estimate how great is the harm that the Church has suffered from the habit of treating poetry as prose, and imagery as science in Theology. But if it be admitted, as in fact is evident, that our Lord, in delineating the spiritual or Immortal Life which He knew intimately, and which no one could know as He knew it, made use of such language as was impotent to express it in its reality, though it was the only language which He could use and His audience comprehend, there can be no doubt as to the need of caution and discrimination in laying stress upon this or that particular word of His teaching.

And further, the language of our Lord has been

transmitted through the Gospels to a late age by the recognised means and agencies of tradition. He spoke, even upon the supreme matters, in the ordinary converse of life. His words were not taken down by shorthand writers. The report of them was not corrected by Himself : so far as appears, it was not referred on any occasion to His authority. The doctrine of Inspiration is among doctrines one of the most difficult; it has never been subjected to definition by the Church ; and any student of Theology who has reflected upon it knows that it is practically impossible to define it in such terms as do not at once incur reasonable criticism. It is natural to believe that "holy men of God spake as they were moved by the Holy Ghost." The Divine Spirit, Whose office it is to inspire human minds with the knowledge of Truth, rested upon the literary labours of the Evangelists. Without His inspiration the Gospels would not have been what they are ; nay, they would not have been at all. But the Evangelists do not claim, and the Gospels, if honestly treated, do not exhibit, a character of complete immunity from fault or error.

It would seem that the Evangelists wrote much as others write. They were not all eye-witnesses of the scenes which they commemorate. They were often dependent upon information. One of them—St. Luke—describes his manner of arriving by inquiry at the truth of events lying beyond his personal knowledge; it is much as any careful and conscientious historian would proceed in composing a secular narrative. Another is himself the subject of dispute; it is not easy to say for certain who he was, and indeed if the truth be told, the Gospel called St. John's looks more like the work of a pupil faithfully recording, to the best of his memory, a master's oral teaching—as the treatises of Aristotle are no doubt in substance the notes of his pupils—than the work of the master himself.

And the Gospels themselves support this theory of their origin. They are not always precise or coincident or uniform. The general impression which they create—the impression of a unique Personality—is the same everywhere; but the details of time and place and circumstance vary. The same conversations are related, but with slight differences. The same incidents occur, but the setting is changed. Everywhere the Gospels produce the effect of honest testimonies given by sincere but variously situated observers or narrators under the ordinary conditions of human knowledge. Nothing in them is stereotyped, nothing formalised. They are spontaneous, not mechanical; they have grown, they are not made. Nobody who is a capable judge of literature doubts that they are true; but their truth lies in the substance, not in the letter; and as authorities they are far more impressive by their discrepancy than if they were only so many copies of the same original.

All this is an argument for treating the Gospels and the other Books of the New Testament in their due measure as evidences for certain broad general conclusions respecting Immortality rather than for any precise and minute theory of the Life Immortal. And this is the treatment which would appear to accord most strictly with the singular reticence which our Lord, as will be seen presently, never failed to observe in speaking of the world behind the veil. For His object was not to satisfy curiosity; it was to stimulate and invigorate the spiritual life.

Now the Christian Revelation, as expressed in the Gospels, may be said to affect both the evidence for Immortality and also the conception or estimate of the Immortal Life. It not only inclines and persuades men to believe that they are Immortal, or, in better words, creates a consciousness of Immortality; but it shows, within certain limits, what Immortality as a state may be properly conceived to be. Both these are matters which demand consideration in this chapter.

Jesus Christ, it has been already said, did not prove Immortality. There is no record of any occasion on which he discussed whether it was probable or not. He took it for granted, as He took the Being of God for granted. It was not an inference, but an axiom of His Gospel. No doubt He was justified in assuming it because His hearers were disposed to admit it. And an assumption, when it is so made, is often more potent, as it is more striking, than proof; for a proof is in general a witness to difference of opinion; but an assumption represents unanimity. Critics of the sacred writings have sometimes imagined that whatever the writers did not prove, or did not assert, they did not believe. The fact is rather the reverse: whatever is proved has been disputed; whatever is asserted has been denied. It is not so much the assertions as the assumptions of the New Testament that represent conviction. For what nobody questions everybody believes. Hence the main articles of the Christian Creed, and especially the Divinity of Our Lord, are seldom enunciated in the New Testament; but they are always and everywhere implied. Jesus Christ made the Immortal, or, as He preferred to call it, "the Eternal Life," an assumption, not a conclusion, of His teaching. He started from it; He did not arrive at it by argument. It was to Him the basis of religion. Upon it rested the superstructure of Christian belief and Christian practice. If it were not true, then all the motives and obligations of Christian duty would fall to the ground. But Jesus Christ's method of treating Immortality was only one instance of His general way of teaching. It was not His wont to reason about truth. He taught "as one having authority." They who believed His Gospel believed not because they were convinced by the validity of the logical evidences submitted to their judgment, but because they knew Him and knew that He would not tell them a lie.

It is well to understand what is the exact force of the evidence which Jesus Christ by this method of teaching could afford to the fact and nature of Immortality.

In the East knowledge does not proceed in

the same manner as in the West. In the Western world it advances by argument. In the Eastern world it advances by authority. Revelation is the voice of authority. It is in its nature didactic and declaratory. It does not persuade, it does not convince, but it compels. A prophet speaking in the name of God does not use syllogisms ; he does not reason from step to step, like a philosopher ; he does not appeal to human intelligence or information ; but he proclaims what he knows to be truth, and he proclaims it with such intense personal emphasis that men must needs listen to his words and obey his admonitions. This is the regular method of Oriental teaching ; it is not argumentative, but authoritative. The proof of the teaching lies not in the weight of external evidences, it lies in the teaching itself ; the teacher declares truth, and declares it upon his personal testimony ; and the conscience of his hearers makes answer that his declaration is true. In a word, all such teaching is an appeal not to the reason, but to the conscience of mankind.

The authoritative teaching of Jesus Christ is naturally elevated above all other such teaching as rests upon authority. It is higher in proportion as His essential Nature is higher than human. For if He was (as He professed to be) the Son of God, if He was One with God, if He came down from God, if it was His merciful Will to teach Mankind, at the cost of personal infinite suffering, truths which it was impossible that they should know unless from Him, then it follows that no voice which has been heard upon earth has spoken like His in the accents of Heaven, nor has it been given to any child of Man as to Him to reveal the things which eye has not seen nor ear heard nor the heart conceived.

Thus it is that Jesus Christ has by His Gospel borne the supreme witness to the soul's Immortality. The doctrine of Immortality has become a Christian doctrine, it has been taken up into the heritage of Christendom; wherever thoughtful cultivated men believe in Immortality, they believe in it now chiefly, or it may be even exclusively, because He believed it and taught it and lived it.

For there are two ways in which a teacher, speaking with authority, may produce or enforce, even among minds addicted to criticism, a persuasion of the truth which he announces. He may recommend the truth by the lucidity and intensity of his conviction, or he may recommend it by the impressiveness of his example.

In both these ways Jesus Christ, above all other teachers, enforced the belief in Immortality.

It has been shown in the second chapter of this essay how great was the historical difficulty of clearing this belief from the material grossness which so long adhered to it. To conceive of the soul as spiritual, *i.e.*, as free from all alloy of matter or substance, has been one of the hardest tasks of the human intellect. Yet it is only when the conception of the soul is so purged, so etherealised, that the belief in its immortal being becomes not merely possible but natural. The great step, then, in recommending Immortality as a belief is to purge the belief of all that materialises or debases it. And Jesus Christ was the first teacher who realised and exhibited the pure spirituality of the soul.

In order to understand His conception of the soul and of the soul's destiny, it is necessary to examine the remarkable phrase which was often upon His lips, as it was also in his heart, "the Eternal Life." To Him this was not something vague or fortuitous, but perfectly definite, not merely *a* life, but *the* life, "the Eternal Life." To Him it was the sole true life, the reality, the substance of which the earthly physical life was, at best, but a shadow. To Him it was the life of one who lived in conscious relation to God. And this life—this Eternal Life—was the life of the soul.

It is in St. John's Gospel that the Eternal Life is set forth most vividly. That Gospel is the most spiritual of the Gospels. It is in a special sense the Gospel of the Lord's Divinity. It dwells, as it were, in an atmosphere of eternity. It is instinct with the thought of "the Eternal Life."

Everywhere it is "the Eternal Life" which is represented as the special boon of Christianity, the unique gift of Jesus Christ to His disciples. What "the Eternal Life" in its nature is will be considered hereafter. One of the greatest commentators upon St. John's writings has justly said that the Eternal Life is "not an endless duration of being, but being of which time is not a measure."[1] For the present it is enough to lay down that it is the life of the soul, and therefore pre-eminently of the spirit. The spiritual life and the Immortal Life are one. "The Eternal Life" is the perfection of the spiritual or Immortal Life. It is the perfected life not of the body, but of the soul. It was the office of Jesus Christ to reveal this life

[1] Westcott, *The Epistles of St. John*, p. 215.

to the world. He revealed it by His teaching and by His example. His disciples not only heard it from His lips, but saw it in His life.

"The Eternal Life"—so He said—was His gift. It was the gift which He alone could bestow. In His final prayer of consecration He uses these words, "Father, the hour is come; glorify Thy Son, that Thy Son also may glorify Thee; as Thou hast given Him power over all flesh, that He should give eternal life to as many as Thou hast given Him."[1]

"The Eternal Life" is the consciousness of the Divine Nature, the communion with the Divine Spirit. "This is life eternal," said the Lord (*i.e.*, "the Eternal Life"), "that they might know Thee the only true God, and Jesus Christ, whom Thou hast sent."[2] Great and solemn are these words. How could He have spoken of knowing God and knowing Himself as the conditions of "the Eternal Life" if He had not wished to "make Himself equal with God"? But, at least, the words show clearly that "the Eternal Life" is a spiritual state.

Yet again "the Eternal Life," as Our Lord declared it, is dependent upon a certain sacramental

[1] St. John xvii. 2.   [2] Ibid. xvii. 3.

relation to Himself. He spoke of it in the mystical language which expressed the intimate union between Christians and Himself. "Verily, verily, I say unto you, except ye eat the flesh of the Son of Man, and drink His blood, ye have no life in you. Whoso eateth My flesh and drinketh My blood hath eternal life; and I will raise him up at the last day."[1]

"The Eternal Life" is thus the note of all His teaching. It is to Him that men come to ask how they may win or inherit that life. He holds in His hands the keys of that life. He announces its conditions and capacities. It is the secret of His Incarnation. It is the benediction of His Spirit. He came into the world that He might impart it to mankind. And when He returns as Judge He will award it as the recompense of faith and virtue. "For God so loved the world, that He gave His only begotten Son, that whosoever believeth in Him should not perish, but have everlasting life" (*i.e.,* "Eternal Life").[2]

It is important that the bearing of this doctrine upon the native Immortality of the soul should be rightly estimated. The Immortal life is the prerogative of all men. The Eternal Life is the prerogative

[1] St. John vi. 53, 54.   [2] Ibid. iii. 16.

of some, but not of all. It is only by a proper discipline of the soul that man becomes endowed with "the Eternal Life."

Man is an immortal being. The soul that is in him cannot die. But the assurance of Immortality, the benediction of Immortality, lies in the cultivation of the highest part of human nature, *i.e.*, of the soul, and pre-eminently of the spirit. When the soul is enlightened by grace, elevated through prayer, and disciplined in sanctity, it attains to its own true and perfect life. That life is "the Life Eternal." And to him who has once apprehended its secret and realised its beatitude, it becomes incomparably better and holier than any boon that the world can give or take away : it is the true life, there is no other life than this.

This is the great revelation of Jesus Christ. He compelled men to believe in Immortality as the supreme truth of their nature by creating in them the sense of a life that could not die.

The conception of a spiritual or Eternal Life as revealed by Jesus Christ descended naturally to the Epistles of the New Testament. It is always regarded as the privilege of Christian faith. If all the souls of men were immortal, as religion taught, it was they alone who had become members of Christ's body that felt this Immortality as an essential law of their being.

Thus St. Paul writes to the Romans, "If Christ be in you, the body is dead because of sin, but the spirit is life because of righteousness"[1]; to the Galatians, "I am crucified with Christ, nevertheless I live; yet not I, but Christ liveth in me"[2]; to the Colossians, "Christ in you, the hope of glory"[3]; to Timothy, in a passage already quoted, that our Saviour Jesus Christ "hath abolished death, and hath brought life and immortality to light through the gospel."[4]

It is always the same thought which occurs, though in different aspects, that Jesus Christ has revealed in His Gospel a new life—a life that is spiritual, immortal and Divine.

It is St. Paul's habit in addressing the Christian Churches whose founder he had been or whose counsellor he was, to employ an expression of which the significance is apt to be obscured, like much else in the Bible, by familiarity. The expression is, "in Christ." A study of his Epistles will

[1] Romans viii. 10.
[2] Galatians ii. 20.
[3] Colossians i. 27.
[4] 2 Timothy i. 10.

show how constantly he so writes. All the relations and activities of the Christian life—its hopes and anxieties, its joys and disappointments, birth, marriage, education, business, amusement, society, suffering, nay, death itself, are regarded as taking place "in Christ." Christ is, as it were, the atmosphere in which the Christian "lives and moves and has his being." And this life "in Christ" though realised or initiated upon earth, is yet essentially a superhuman, supernatural life. For to be "in Christ," to be one with Christ is, as St. Paul held, to possess the secret of eternity.

Jesus Christ, then, revealed Man to himself. He saw and declared what was Man's true nature. He drew him out of low carnal desires and appetites, and set his feet upon the high ground of eternity. "Alone in all history," as Emerson says, "He estimated the greatness of Man."[1] And, as in Revelation generally, so in this, its paramount article, the conscience of Humanity made an immediate response to the appeal of the Divine Master. When He pronounced the Immortality of the human spirit, when He declared the necessity of so cultivating

[1] Address delivered before the Senior Class in Divinity College, Cambridge, Massachusetts.

and disciplining the spirit that it should ascend to the realisation of its own eternal and unfading power, the men and women who sat at His feet became conscious of a new sentiment that was itself an inspiration.

It was said of Lord Chatham that he breathed a new spirit into the people of England. His presence inspired them; his voice was as a trumpet-call in their ears. They who heard him became new men; they felt themselves capable of nobler and more exalted actions. His words evoked a burning patriotism. The patriotic sentiment existed already in their hearts, but it was he who could give it life, energy and virtue. Similarly (if it be not irreverent to make the comparison), but in a far higher sense, did Jesus Christ evoke the sentiment of Immortality. He taught men to know themselves—to know their true nature. Without His teaching men felt and owned themselves to be Immortal; but their Immortality was not the paramount fact of their being; it was in the Gospel that human Immortality assumed such importance as to overshadow all the interests and ambitions of the present life.

It is thus that Jesus Christ, above all other teachers, has stamped the fact of Immortality upon the heart and conscience of the world. He took the Immortal or Eternal Life as the basis of His revelation. He laid His finger upon Man's spiritual faculty as the seat and source of Immortality. He showed how that faculty might be raised to its true and rightful supremacy in human nature. And He made men feel that it was in virtue of their capacity for "the Eternal Life" that they stood in the relation of closest affinity to their Maker. And with His conception of "the Eternal Life" agreed His supreme sense of the value attaching to the soul as contrasted with all external joys or endowments. This, as the highest point of all teaching in regard to the soul, has been set forth in the second chapter of this Essay, where the history of the belief in Immortality was considered. Jesus Christ changed, as it were, the centre of gravity in human nature by insisting upon the awful and unique moment of the soul. For when He asked, "What shall it profit a man if he shall gain the whole world and lose his own soul? or what shall a man give in exchange for his soul?" or again when He bade His disciples fear not one whose power was limited to killing the body, but him alone who had power to kill the soul, His words could not fail, nor did they fail in fact, to create and intensify the consciousness of a spiritual life, or a life of the soul, so vital and valuable that in comparison with it the bodily life became as nothing. And it was this realisation of the soul's eternal value that was felt to be the most impressive witness to Immortality.

But it is not only by the strong conviction of the Eternal Life as the great reality, or even by the insistence upon the paramount dignity of the soul as the seat or centre of that life, that Jesus Christ revealed eternity to mankind. There is a teaching more impressive than any words. It is the teaching of example ; and He not only preached the Eternal Life, but He lived it. He was Himself His Revelation. He was the Way, and the Truth, but above all the Life. The greatest of all witnesses to Immortality is not Christ's teaching, nor His creative work in the Church of the ages, nor even His Resurrection : it is Christ.

The argument of His example may be put in this way :

Jesus Christ was Man. He was Man as truly as any human being that breathes. He assumed human nature in its integrity. Although He ennobled that nature by its union with Divinity, it remained essentially human.

But Humanity is a unit. It deserves to be regarded as a whole. It possesses its own corporate character, its own collective individuality. All men, therefore, in the essential points of human nature, are alike. Differences of time, race, locality, &c.,are accidental; the similarity is vital. It follows that any attainment or achievement of one man elevates mankind. Whatever Man has done, Man may aspire to do. Whatever Man has been, Man may hope to become. The most convincing proof of human spirituality is that one human being should have lived a Life entirely spiritual. And if that Life was the highest ever lived upon earth, it is sufficient in itself to declare and demonstrate the supremacy of the spiritual element in Humanity. For spirituality, as has been said, is the promise and the witness of the Life Immortal and Eternal.

Alone among the sons of men Jesus Christ lived upon earth "the Eternal Life" in its complete integrity. He is therefore the one man whose life affords a perfect assurance of Immortality.

To estimate His Divine Life in any full measure would be alien from the purpose of this Essay. But no one will deny that its characteristic was spirituality. It was not, like other lives, broken and marred, but a seamless robe, perfect in its communion with the Divine.

Jesus Christ cared for one object uniquely. His pure soul was not distracted by conflicting ambitions. The common interests of life—wealth, rank, culture, advancement—were little in His eyes. He was poor, homeless and alone. The one ambition of His Life was goodness. "My meat," He said, "is to do the Will of Him that sent Me and to finish His work."[1] He came to save the world.

It is this absolute devotion to a spiritual object which separates His Life from all other lives in the world's history. His is the one completely religious life. It is the one life in which the true end of human being is pursued without any hesitancy, without any failing, from first to last.

When we consider what that Life is as it appears to us who can look upon it only through the darkening vista of centuries, we can faintly realise how His intimate friends, who were its eye-witnesses, must have been moved and influenced by it. It is so different from most human lives, though common eyes could see no difference. It is a Life unearthly, Divine. It is holy and immaculate. The taint of

[1] St. John iv. 34.

sin, that ever clings about the best and saintliest of human characters, is impotent to touch Him; it cannot rest upon Him, cannot come nigh Him; His Presence forbids it, and it is as though, while walking on earth, He breathed the air, the pure and serene atmosphere that lies around the throne of God in Heaven.

What, then, was the effect of that Divine Life upon those who knew and loved it?

It was to produce an absolute conviction of Immortality.

The faithful friends of Christ's Life could not believe that it ended when His body was laid in the grave. They felt that He had displayed before human eyes the witness of a spiritual and ageless existence. And they humbly hoped that, as partakers of His Nature, they would, according to His promise, share His Immortality.

The late Master of Balliol puts in beautiful words the influence of such a Life as Jesus Christ's upon the affectionate and appreciative hearts of His disciples. "The belief in a future life," he says, "is not derived from Revelation, though greatly strengthened by it. It is the growing sense of human nature respecting itself. And this sense of a future life and judgment to come has been so quickened in us by Christianity that it may be said almost to have been created by it. It is the witness of Christ Himself, than which to the Christian no assurance can be greater. He who meditates on this Divine Life in the brief narrative which has been preserved of it, will find the belief in another world come again to him when many physical and metaphysical proofs are beginning to be as broken reeds. He will find more than enough to balance the difficulties of the manner 'how' or the time 'when.' He will find, as he draws nearer to Christ, a sort of impossibility of believing otherwise." [1]

But the eye-witnesses of Christ's Life realised not only that He was Immortal, but that they were themselves Immortal too. As they looked upon "the Eternal Life" manifested in Him and saw it to consist in His purity, His spirituality, His communion with God, His perfect obedience to the Divine Will, it dawned upon them that they too, in such measure as they drew near to Him, would become capable of such an "Eternal Life" as His.

[1] Quoted by Dr. Salmond, *The Christian Doctrine of Immortality*, p. 393.

For "the Eternal Life" was not only His possession; it was His gift. And He could give it in virtue of His relation to the whole human family.

In Christian Theology that relation has been often drawn out in rather precise and definite language. It follows in the main the lines of St. Paul's original argument in the 15th chapter of the first Epistle to the Corinthians. It need not be here considered except in so far as it bears upon the witness of Christ's Person to the doctrine of human Immortality.

Christ, it may be said, is the archetypal man. He is, in St. Paul's words, "the second Adam," *i.e.*, He stands to all Humanity in a similar or parallel relation to that in which the first Adam stands to the same Humanity. In more precise language, as the heritage of Adam's sin passed by the law of Nature to all Adam's posterity, so to the same posterity by the same law of Nature passes the heritage of Christ's perfect spirituality. "As in Adam all die, even so in Christ shall all be made alive."

St. Paul confines his argument to the Resurrection; but it is equally true of Immortality. The peculiar relation of Jesus Christ to the human family creates the probability—it may almost be called the certainty—that, if He established His own Immortality, He established it not for Himself alone but for all who are participant in the nature that He took upon Himself.

Jesus Christ, then, by His personal example, revealed the Immortal, or, more properly, the Eternal Life as the prerogative of human nature. Living Himself, as a man, a life that was instinctively felt to be incapable of death, He imprinted upon mankind the strong assurance that the soul of Man could not perish, but should live eternally. "The Eternal Life" is the perfection of Immortality. It is the Immortal Life spent in the consciousness of God. It is—if an inadequate illustration may be forgiven, where none could be adequate—it is to mere unsanctified or unspiritualised Immortality as a life enriched with the graces, embellishments and dignities of culture is to the life of primitive barbarism. It is the sole true or perfect life. It is the life which alone realises Man's proper nature. "The Eternal Life" is the spiritual Immortal Life in its highest form.

And this was the Life which Jesus Christ lived upon earth. He lived it upon the earth; but it was an unearthly life, as it rose above the material circumstances of common Humanity. He lived, as it were, in the clear air of a mountain-height, while others, living at its feet, were in mist and darkness. Upon Him, and upon Him alone among the sons of men, the light of Heaven shone uncloudedly. And so it was given to Him to teach the world that the true life of Man consists not in the "things that he possesseth," nor in aught that is carnal or sensuous, but in peace and purity and communion with God. In a word, Jesus Christ lived absolutely and uniformly the life which men live partially and fitfully, if they live it at all. His Life was the actual manifestation of the Divine Nature to human eyes. Thus He could say, "He that hath seen Me hath seen the Father."[1] But as God is Spirit, the Divine Life is wholly spiritual, and the Life which is wholly spiritual is immortal; it cannot die.

Thus the testimony of Jesus Christ to Immortality is the testimony of His teaching and of His example. But it is by His example that He taught most powerfully. It has been the Will of God to regenerate the world by the exhibition of a Divine Character. Jesus Christ in His very Nature is the

[1] St. John xiv. 9.

source of the highest beliefs and aspirations of Humanity. Men believe in Immortality because they believe in Him. It is the privilege, as has been already said, of sanctified souls, wherever they occur, to create a belief in their own Immortality. They possess in themselves the secret of Eternal Life. They reveal a potency transcending and surviving experience. The human mind in the observation of such souls feels an instinctive, ineradicable assurance that they pass through the gate of death into a larger and more spiritual existence. And of such souls Jesus Christ as Man is the chief.

But when it is admitted that the Life of Jesus is the surest witness of eternity, it remains to consider and, as far as possible, to determine what was the nature of His teaching in regard to the future life. For not only did He assume human Immortality and constitute it as the basis of His Revelation, but He showed in some sense what the Immortal or Eternal Life would be. Here and there in the New Testament, and in the Gospels especially, are suggestive hints and intimations—sidelights thrown, as it were, upon the future of souls; and to gather these up and compare and interpret them is part of the true work of Christian exegesis.

Revelation, then, affects both the evidence for Immortality and also the conception of the Immortal Life.

It is necessary, indeed, according to the principle already laid down, to observe great caution in drawing inferences from scattered phrases and passages even of our Lord's own teaching. And not only so; but His teaching upon futurity must be treated as a whole. Any exaggeration or disproportion of one part may mar the whole picture. We will try to be faithful to His words.

Immortality is the prerogative of Man as Man. It is an element of the dignity attaching to human nature as being made in the image of the Godhead. Our Lord in one memorable passage deduces it from the relation of God as Himself Immortal to His creatures. "God is not a God of the dead, but of the living, for all live unto Him."[1]

Immortality (so far as experience tells) begins at birth. "The Eternal Life" is the perfect realisation of Immortality. It is the Immortal Life as lived in conscious intimate relation to God. It begins not at birth but at baptism. "The Eternal Life" as revealed by Christ, does not begin at death

[1] St. Luke xx. 38.

or after death. He speaks of "having" or "not having" the Eternal Life as a present reality. No doubt, as that life is itself the evidence of Immortality, it must be conceived as transcending death; it is immortal, it is perpetual; but it does not begin at death; it begins, or it may begin, here and now. As Man's Immortality, so too his "Eternal Life" is not only future, but present.

It is true, as will presently appear, that death breaks down the sensuous barriers which cramp and confine the pure activity of the spirit during the period of the present earthly life. The spirit of one in whom "the Eternal Life" is realised becomes at death emancipated and ennobled. It enters upon the future with new powers. In its state of felicity it must be regarded as attaining after death to visions, revelations, enjoyments, ecstasies of which it is incapable, or at the most only in part capable, during life.

It may be said in general that Protestant Theology has tended to make too much of death. There is no warrant in Holy Scripture for the assumption that death is an absolute dividing-line between one state and another; still less, that on one side of the line all is preparation, and on the other all is recompense or penalty. The Christian view of death is not that it is the end of life, but that it is an event—the most important of all events—in life.

For if it be true that "the Eternal Life" begins in this life, not less true is it that the life which is the opposite of the eternal—the life which is the profanation of the spiritual part of Man's nature, as "the Eternal Life" is its consecration—begins in this life; and death does not make an absolute abrupt change in human nature or in the relation of human nature to the Divine; it is not the cessation of life, but its continuation, only in immaterial or purely spiritual conditions.

What, then, is the change affected by death in human nature?

According to the Christian view the body perishes or is dissolved at death; the soul survives. It survives in all its powers, intellectual, moral and spiritual. It carries with it into futurity the weight of its guilt and shame and suffering; it carries also its prerogative of duty achieved and character disciplined by patience and faith won at the foot of the Cross.

It is because death does not in a moment reverse or undo the effect of the earthly life that that life gains inexpressible importance. Although it would be wrong, upon the argument of this Essay, to emphasise particular points in our Lord's Revelation of Immortality, there can be no doubt that He taught the supreme value of the present life as affecting the future destiny of mankind. To Him the one thing hateful, the one thing fatal, was sin; but sin was a taint contracted in the present life; and to purge away the taint of sin was a task so difficult as to demand a Divine Sacrifice. No doubt it was in His power to announce an immediate blessing, as to the dying thief on the Cross, to one who placed an implicit faith in His Divinity. Such a blessing so announced is infinitely precious, as it forbids the shutting of the door of hope against any sinner; but it stands alone in the New Testament; it does not contravene the general Divine law of dealing with souls.

Jesus Christ laid down the principle of retribution. He taught that sin in its nature implied and involved punishment. Punishment must attend evil, as the shadow attends a man. "The soul that sinneth it shall die." If it is not always apparent in this life that suffering is the necessary result of sin, it is because in this life there are temporal conditions interposing between cause and consequence in the Providential order. But it is as sure as the sequence of night upon day that every violation of the Divine law carries in itself an ultimate pain ; it must be purged away by fire.

For sin, as Jesus Christ viewed it, is not mere failure, misfortune or error, not mere human infirmity, a mark for tolerance or compassion (although this view of it is not so much erroneous as inadequate), it is an affront to the Majesty of God ; and, as being such, it excites in a pure and righteous mind—and how much more in the Divine Mind !—a sentiment of indignation or abhorrence, a burning flame which cannot be quenched until the sin is done away. And Jesus Christ associated the law of the Divine Justice with an event which should be the consummation of the world's History and the vindication of God's Providence, viz., His own future Advent in Glory. "The Son of Man shall come in His glory, and all the holy angels with Him." Then shall the sentence of eternal felicity or eternal punishment be spoken to "all nations." Then shall the severance of the sheep from the goats take its effect. That the ground of reward shall be charity and the ground of condemnation shall be hardness of heart is well known : it accords with the Christian estimate of righteousness and sin as the two essential factors in human life; but, however pictorial the scene may be as portrayed in the Gospel, it brings out in strong light that it is for the "deeds done in the body" that men shall be judged at the Judgment Seat of Christ.

Beyond the declaration of retributory Immortality, beyond the declaration of the paramount moral character attaching to human life, it does not appear to me that the words of our Lord may justly be taken as reaching. The imagination of physical horrors in the unseen world belongs to His followers in later ages but not to Him; it is Theology, it is not the Gospel. It is a sore pity that theologians should have imported their hatred or their spite into His Revelation. They have forgotten that He spoke "in parables," that He made use of metaphorical and tropical language, that it was His intention to express the awful significance of human life, human sin and human destiny, by a few broad emphatic touches, but not in detail.

After all, His language must be read in the light of common sense—nay, I would rather say, of Divine charity. Revelation informs, it does not crush, the moral consciousness of Humanity. God is—He must be—better than His children.

> "That one unquestioned text we read
> All doubt beyond, all fear above,
> Nor crackling pile, nor cursing creed
> Can burn or blot it: God is LOVE."[1]

To come back to the teaching of Jesus Christ: It is evident that, while He asserted a difference in the future destinies of the good and the evil, and this a difference conditioned by their human lives, He observed a singular reticence in His delineations of the future invisible life, whether of suffering or of felicity. Nothing in the Gospels is more striking than His constant reserve upon the matters which He might perhaps have been expected to elucidate. Other teachers of religion—Mohammed, especially—chose to present the future fate of souls in colours the most vivid and impressive. But Jesus Christ seemed expressly to aim at subordinating the natural curiosity of men respecting the future to practical immediate interests and duties of the present.

It is possible, I think, to suggest a reason for this reserve. When the future life engrosses and absorbs the thoughts of the world, men are apt to become neglectful of common obligations. In the Epistles of the New Testament St. Paul, who believed in the

---

[1] O. W. Holmes.

near approach of the Day of Judgment, is careful to warn his Christian converts against the disturbing and distracting nature of such a belief; he urges it habitually as a motive, not to extravagance or fanaticism, but to a disciplined self-command and self-control. There were critical periods of the Middle Ages when nations flung aside the restraints of order and morality under the conviction that the day of the Lord was at hand. Our Lord's express warning that He would come "as a thief in the night" was plainly intended to create vigilance, but to prohibit excitement. "Of that day and that hour knoweth no man, no, not the angels which are in heaven, neither the Son, but the Father."[1] The sober practical performance of duty in the visible life as a preparation for the invisible is the temper characteristic of Christianity.

Now if our Lord had willed to set forth in vivid detail the whole scope and manner and condition of the future life, the effect would have been to overshadow in men's eyes the present life, to make it seem insignificant, indeed contemptible, and to produce in men a wholly unpractical habit of mind. They would have lived as enthusiasts or as hermits,

[1] St. Mark xiii. 32.

not as sensible and serious citizens. And this danger—great in itself—would have been the greater, if He had deigned to reveal the nature of the punitive processes by which the sin-stained soul is redeemed.

Thus it is, or seems to be, that such Revelation as our Lord affords of the unseen world refers almost wholly to the world of light. He speaks of Heaven; the darkness of Hell He leaves to be inferred by the law of contrast. It is in accordance with His Mind, then, to inquire more nearly what Heaven will be; it is not so to speculate upon Hell. But even here His singular reticence does not fail. It is the more remarkable, because in the Gospels He claims to possess a perfect knowledge of the heavenly state. If He does not tell what Heaven is, it is not that He does not know, it is that He does not will to tell.

Jesus Christ, as has been said, assumed the fact of Immortality. He impressed it upon human hearts by the doctrine of "the Eternal Life" which He exemplified. And He declared that of "the Eternal Life," when set free from material limitations, He knew, and He alone, the absolute truth.

Jesus Christ was as intimately acquainted with

Heaven as any one may be with the scene of his earthly home. In all that He says of it His words are stamped with complete information and authority. His words are such as these, "In My Father's house are many mansions; if it were not so, I would have told you. I go to prepare a place for you."[1] "They neither marry nor are given in marriage, but are as the angels of God in heaven."[2] "Take heed that ye despise not one of these little ones; for I say unto you that in heaven their angels do always behold the face of My Father which is in heaven."[3] "I say unto you, There is joy in the presence of the angels of God over one sinner that repenteth."[4] "To-day shalt thou be with me in Paradise."[5] "No man hath seen God at any time; the only begotten Son, which is in the bosom of the Father, He hath declared Him."[6]

These and other such passages, however some of them may be interpreted, are clear and definite in their assertion of a complete knowledge respecting Heaven and the heavenly state.

No doubt the language of our Lord is figurative or allegorical, and it must be interpreted with due

---

[1] St. John xiv. 2. [2] St. Matthew xxii. 30. [3] St. Matthew xviii. 10.
[4] St. Luke xv. 10. [5] St. Luke xxiii. 43. [6] St. John i. 18.

regard to its character. For the heavenly life is in its nature purely spiritual. It is the life of the spirit —of the soul—not of the body. It is free from material conditions; for spirit is not matter, but the opposite of matter, and therefore whatever conditions are necessary or natural to matter are or may be assumed to be alien from spirit.

Human thought is impotent to apprehend spiritual existence. So far as existence falls within human observation, it is always material. It is subject to material limitations. We do not speak of spiritual or intellectual life except under metaphor. Such words as "comprehension" or "apprehension" are themselves metaphorical; so too are all words relating to the mind or the soul. The inherent difficulty of metaphysics is that metaphysical language is physical language used in an artificial significance.

How, then, is it possible to impress upon human minds, confined as they are within materialistic limits, a conception of a life that is immaterial, spiritual, eternal? There is no other way than the use of material language; but to accept such language literally is to misunderstand it. Our Lord, in portraying the life of Heaven used, and could not avoid using, a terminology derived from the life of earth.[1]

Thus He spoke of Heaven in the language of place. He called it "paradise." When He would describe the future blessedness of emancipated souls, He said it was to "lie in Abraham's bosom," employing a Rabbinical phrase which His hearers could hardly mistake. The "many mansions" of Heaven are not actual edifices; no reasonable person would think of so understanding them; they indicate the character of Heaven, not its structure.

In the *Apocalypse* again "the holy city, New Jerusalem" which St. John saw "coming down from God out of heaven, prepared as a bride adorned for her husband" is described, in respect of its walls and its foundations and its gates, nay, of its dimensions, with a precise and elaborate accuracy which simply forbids the idea of literal interpretation.

Such language, intelligently and reverently considered, deserves to be placed beside the parables

---

[1] In the part of the Essay beginning here I have employed and in some degree extended the argument of a contribution which I made some little time ago to a book entitled *The Faith of Centuries*.

of our Lord Himself. For they too are vivid representations of spiritual laws under the aspect of natural phenomena; and while no attempt at literal precision would or could have wrought a hundredth part of the effect that the parables have wrought upon the conscience of the world, it would be an error to forget that they are broad spiritual pictures, not to be treated scientifically or to be pressed in every detail, but Divine suggestions and adumbrations of truths that lie, and must for ever lie, beyond the reach of Man's unsanctified intelligence.

Similarly our Lord spoke of Heaven in the language of time. Immortality, Eternity are not indeed strictly temporal expressions. They are the negation of time, not its prolongation; but as existence apart from time does not fall under human experience, it is commonly, although unphilosophically, regarded as illimitable time, which is itself a self-contradiction, an unthinkable thought.

It is not to be denied that our Lord spoke of the future life, or of the life which reaches into futurity although it is a present life, as "æonian" or eternal, or that His apostles spoke of it as lasting "for ever and ever," *i.e.*, more strictly "for ages of ages." Nor is this language to be explained or

AMPLIFICATION OF THE BELIEF

whittled away; the life is "æonian" and the punishment endured within it "æonian"; but it is the language of earth applied to the life of Heaven or of Hell; it is material language but not spiritual, and it must not be understood as though it were possible to convey under the forms of material existence a precise idea of such a life as is absolutely and intrinsically free from all association with matter.

Heaven—and Hell too, as its shadow—is not a place or a time, but a *state*. It is not subject to any conditions, local or temporal. It is not here or now, but simply *is;* and the truest thought of it, is to think of it in itself without any such question as where it is or when or for how long.

Our Lord always described "the Eternal Life" in relation to God. Man in his probation upon earth possesses a certain spiritual affinity to his Maker. The affinity is circumscribed by material conditions. But Man in his felicity, however it may be attained, will enjoy a perfect intimacy with God. Then will his human nature be fully assimilated to the Divine. And in virtue of this assimilation, progressive or final, Man's life—his "Eternal Life"—will put off the conditions of the flesh, *i.e.*, of time and place and of matter generally, and will become wholly spiritual ; it will be, in our Lord's own language, as the life of the angels.

To spiritualise the conception of the Divine Nature and so of human nature as the image of the Divine was the lesson of our Lord in His Revelation. But it is when we realise, as far as Man may, what the spirit is and the spiritual life and all that belongs to it that we understand how solemn the duty of caution is in speculating and deciding upon the invisible world.

This one fact, however, is certain, that, as death is the separation of body and soul, or in other words, of the material and spiritual elements in human nature, whatever impediment the body or the flesh sets to the activity of the soul or to its passivity must be assumed to be done away at death.

For instance, it is the Divine law that sin should entail suffering. That law, like other similar laws, is not completely but only partially vindicated in the present life. To realise it as absolute and universal is an act of faith. We see in part, we know in part. There are sinful actions which are seen to be attended by immediate or ultimate punishment in the present life. The drunkard or the debauchee bears often, if not invariably, upon his person the visible marks of the Divine anger against sin. It is not so with all sinful actions. There are actions which, however antagonistic they may be to God's Will, are not evidently followed by temporal punishment. Still more there are virtuous actions which seem to issue in loss and suffering. All this has been felt, and in this essay has been urged, as an argument for the belief in Immortality. But when it is asked, What is it that interposes between virtue and its satisfaction, between sin and its penalty? the answer, if briefly put, is—the flesh. It is because the soul of Man in his earthly life is not free and open to the laws of Providence, but is, as it were, enveloped, hardened and concealed by matter, *i.e.*, by the flesh, that he does not feel, or feels only imperfectly, the Divinely appointed sequence of cause and effect in good and evil. But let the material veil be rent asunder, as it will be at death, and let the soul of Man stand face to face with his Maker; then will the Divine blessing and the Divine indignation be realised in their fulness and, as the guilty will at once experience an anguish of which they were unconscious and incapable upon earth, so will the righteous, when they "awake after God's likeness," be enriched with the fruition of a felicity such as the world can neither give nor take away.

In the light of this thought the intimations of Jesus Christ respecting Immortality became infinitely significant. They may be drawn from His own words and from the words of His inspired Apostles.

The soul, it has been said, which survives the hour of death is equivalent to the total sum of the intellectual, moral and spiritual powers of human nature. All these powers, then, are carried into Eternity. All are emancipated from the limiting and obscuring influence of matter. And all are by this emancipation quickened, energised and intensified.

Thus the intellect of Man, in its relation to Divine Providence, is confronted by serious difficulties. As it looks out upon the face of Nature, it stands bewildered. The world is not what it might naturally be expected to be upon the supposition of an Omnipotent and Benevolent Creator. It is in St. Paul's phrase "made subject to vanity." It lies under gloom, contradiction and apparent failure. The intellect of Man is for ever asking why things are ordered as they are and not otherwise, what is their law or purport or end. Among the facts of human thought none is more striking—none more significant

—than the tenacity with which Man, when once he has attained to the belief in God has clung to it amidst a thousand difficulties and disappointments.

The Christian theological view is that the intellect of Man is not, nor can be, a competent critic of Divine Providence. It is limited in the same way as his eyesight; and it can be aided by faith as his eyesight by the microscope or the telescope. But so long as Man remains in the flesh, so long must it be impossible for him to understand the ways of God. There is always a veil spread, as it were, between him and his Maker; he sees "through a glass, darkly," he knows only "in part," it is behind the veil that he shall see "face to face," and shall "know even as he is known."

For if the flesh, with its varied appetites and affections, is upon the whole the curtain which dims the light of Heaven, it is a natural inference that, when the curtain is done away by the emancipation of the spirit from the flesh, the light will shine in its full radiancy upon the soul. Then will doubts and difficulties cease. Then will faith be unimpeded and unclouded. Then will the soul contemplate the celestial verities as they are in themselves.

The student of the Apocalypse will recall the

splendid scene in which it is related how "the book written within and on the backside, sealed with seven seals" is opened. "And no man in heaven, nor on earth, neither under the earth, was able to open the book, neither to look thereon. And I wept much," says the Divine seer, "because no man was found worthy to open and to read the book, neither to look therein. And one of the elders said unto me, Weep not, behold the Lion of the tribe of Juda, the Root of David, hath prevailed to open the book, and to loose the seven seals thereof."[1] What is the purport of the scene, if it be not that in the eternal world the ever-present, ever-haunting mystery of Creation will at length be revealed? The redeemed souls will enjoy the beatific vision. They will meditate, with ineffable wonder and awe, upon the Providential plan extending from eternity to eternity. They will discern in the Incarnation of the Son of God the solution of all that was dark and hopeless in men's eyes before that event and even since has been known and reverenced only "in part." And as they realise the infinite majesty and mercy of the Divine Plan, encompassing, as it shall, the whole Creation, animate and inanimate, they shall burst into the

[1] Revelation v. 3–5.

exultant anthem which the seer heard to issue from
"ten thousand times ten thousand, and thousands of
thousands." "Worthy is the Lamb that was slain
to receive power, and riches and wisdom, and
strength and honour and glory and blessing. . . .
Blessing and honour and glory and power, be unto
Him, that sitteth upon the throne, and unto the
Lamb for ever and ever."[1]

But the thought of the unseen world suggests a
moral as well as an intellectual illumination. And
this too depends upon the emancipation of the soul
from the trammels of the flesh. For the flesh, as
St. Paul regards it, is the centre of the anti-spiritual
affections and passions in human nature. For "the
flesh lusteth against the spirit, and the spirit against
the flesh, and these are contrary the one to the other.
So that ye cannot do the things that ye would."[2]
And again, "To be carnally minded (*i.e.*, the mind
of the flesh, τὸ φρόνημα τῆς σαρκός) is death; but to
be spiritually minded (i.e., the mind of the spirit,
τὸ φρόνημα τοῦ πνεύματος) is life and peace."[3]

In fact, the New Testament consistently represents
two main forces as antagonistic to the moral or

---

[1] Revelation v. 12, 13. [2] Galatians v. 17.
[3] Romans viii. 6.

spiritual life which Christ enjoined ; and both are intimately associated with matter.

One is the world—the κόσμος, properly the ordered visible Universe, the opposite of Chaos, but taken by our Lord and by His Apostles after Him to signify the total sum of the secular or material interests, influences, occupations and associations which tend to come between the soul of Man and God. This it is which our Lord treated as His main enemy ; it was this which nailed Him to the Cross. To save men from the world was the object of His life and of His death. Thus He said, " If the world (ὁ κόσμος) hate you, ye know that it hated Me before it hated you. If ye were of the world, the world would love his own ; but because ye are not of the world, but I have chosen you out of the world, therefore the world hateth you."[1] And soon afterwards, "In the world (ἐν τῷ κόσμῳ) ye shall have tribulation ; but be of good cheer, I have overcome the world."[2] So too, St. John in a remarkable passage which reflects the specially Christian tone of thought respecting the material world, uses these words, "Love not the world (τὸν κόσμον), neither the things that are in the world. If any man love the world, the love of the

---

[1] St. John xv. 19. [2] Ibid. xvi. 33.

Father is not in him. For all that is in the world, the lust of the flesh, and the lust of the eyes and the pride of life, is not of the Father, but is of the world. And the world passeth away, and the lust thereof; but he that doeth the will of God abideth for ever."[1]

The world, then, or κόσμος, is the material Universe. Sometimes, as in the passage of St. John's Epistle, it includes the lower or sensual side of human nature, "the lust of the flesh, and the lust of the eyes," but it is not so used generally. "The world," strictly considered, stands for all that in external Nature tells against sanctity or against spirituality, for all that is contrary to the Will of God. But all this is essentially material; its sphere is the visible or tangible or substantial; it is different and distant from what is spiritual.

The other anti-spiritual force is the flesh (ἡ σάρξ). And as "the world" is used for all such material objects as, lying outside the nature of Man, do yet in their measure and degree draw him away from God, so is "the flesh" used for the material and secular tendencies of his nature itself. Christian souls know only too well what this power of "the flesh" is. For, as they feel after God and aspire to

[1] 1 St. John ii. 15-17.

Him, they are sorrowfully conscious of something within them that impedes and degrades their higher being, something that drags them back as with chains irresistible, and thwarts the nobility and sanctity that is in them, and compels or inclines them to do what they hate and contemn themselves for doing. How true to life is St. Paul's confession—as true as it is graphic! "I delight in the law of God after the inward man. But I see another law in my members, warring against the law of my mind, and bringing me into captivity to the law of sin which is in my members. O wretched man that I am! Who shall deliver me from the body of this death?"[1]

But it is important to observe that this influence of evil is by St. Paul conceived as essentially material. His words, "the law of sin which is in my members," "the body of this death," as elsewhere, "the mind of the flesh," point to matter as the seat and centre of evil. And is it not a simple fact of human experience that besides the devil and the world there is in Man an influence drawing him away from God—an influence of which he is conscious in all the difficulties and

[1] Romans vii. 22-24.

embarrassments of his moral life—and that the seat of this influence is the sense or the body, the material part of his composite being; in one word, the "flesh"? But if this be so, it follows that the emancipation of the soul from the body at death will be, at least in the instance of the blessed souls, a deliverance from the lowering, humiliating tendency of matter, whether in the world or in the flesh. The soul will no more experience a constant antinomy. It will no more approve one thing and do another, no more act as it would fain not have acted, no more see the vision of beauty and forget or neglect it. Moral duty will become clear and commanding. It will speak in imperious and irresistible tones. It will be freed from the pains and difficulties which now attend it; for as it is the association of the soul with the body that in the present life renders the performance of duty difficult and painful, so when the soul is set free from the body it will realise at last the perfect and cloudless felicity of doing the Will of God as a simple pleasure continually without any hindrance at all or failure or distress.

Such, then, in its moral aspect is "the Eternal Life" as our Lord taught it, the pure spiritual life, the life of Heaven. Such too was the lesson of His own Life, as when He said, "Wist ye not that I must be about my Father's business?"[1] or "My meat is to do the Will of Him that sent Me and to finish His work,"[2] or again, "I do always those things that please Him."[3] For indeed He lived on earth the heavenly life; and to do the Will of God perfectly and to be perfectly happy in doing it is Heaven. This is the life for which Man, as redeemed by Christ, is permitted to look. It will be to him a restoration, a regeneration. His moral nature, clouded as it has been upon earth, shall become purified. As the saints upon earth—the souls who stand nearest to God—have many a time found happiness and peace unspeakable, amidst most bitter sufferings of the flesh, in doing God's Will; so shall the redeemed and sanctified souls in Heaven experience what it is to toil without effort or reluctance, and to serve without weariness, and to fulfil the moral law of their being in complete felicity, knowing God even as they are known of Him.

But the life of Heaven, if it is intellectual, if it is moral, is also spiritual or devotional—nay, it is this above all else. And that it must be so is evident

---

[1] St. Luke ii. 49. [2] St. John iv. 34. [3] St. John viii. 29.

in the nature of things. For what is the true attitude of Man toward his Maker? It is not reflexion, still less is it criticism; it is worship.

The proper dignity of Man lies in worship. Humility is his honour. Prostration before the throne of the Supreme is his exaltation. It is not when he gives himself airs as though he were lord of the visible Universe, but when he cries, standing afar off, "God be merciful to me a sinner," that he rises to the true height of his nature. Higher than the hero, higher than the philosopher is, in the standard of Divine realities, the saint.

Yet to Man upon earth it is almost infinitely difficult to enter upon his right relation to his Maker. He does not know God. He does not know even himself. His opinion of his own place in Nature is, as has been said, at one time too high, at another too low. Were it not for special experiences such as suffering, bereavement, and death, or again such as moments of ecstasy and inspiration, he would not feel that he was or could be a son of God.

And even when he realises the duty and blessing of worshipping God, how much is there that comes between him and the heavenly vision!

There is no such humbling fact of human nature as that Man cannot even worship as he would. His supplications, his adorations are always imperfect. His very prayers need to be prayed over again. His penitences need themselves to be repented of. It is this fact which makes the spiritual life even of the best men a spectacle so pathetic, so tragical.

And yet man feels within himself a longing after God, a power of communion with God. Nothing can wholly destroy or disguise it. It is an element of his humanity. It is a witness to his capacity for "the Eternal Life." "The spirit itself beareth witness with our spirit, that we are the children of God."[1]

But when it is asked what are the causes that make Man, in his earthly life, only half-conscious of his affinity to God, or only half-capable of Divine worship, the answer must inevitably be that they lie in the material or carnal appetites and tendencies of his nature, *i.e.*, in the flesh. Thus it is that in his best moments he longs above all else to be freed from the flesh. He desires to become a pure spiritual being, as are the angels who do

[1] Romans viii. 16.

God's Will perfectly. It would seem, then, that the condition of spirituality is the emancipation of the soul from the body. For "flesh and blood cannot inherit the kingdom of God,"[1] as St. Paul says. But this is just the change which death effects; and such a change, unless it be vitiated by a personal taint, *e.g.*, by sin, as it places Man in direct relation to his Maker, will necessarily elicit his full energy of admiring and adoring veneration. When we see God as He is, we shall worship Him as we ought.

While it would be a speculative error then, and in some sense a detraction from the full Christian doctrine of Immortality, to imagine that "the Eternal Life" beyond the grave will be wholly devotional, and while it is a part of the Christian Revelation to believe that that life will afford scope for the intellectual and moral excellences of which human nature is capable, as well as for the devotional, yet the whole tenour of Christ's teaching implies that worship will be the soul's most potent and persistent exercise in futurity. We shall know then, not partially, as now, but fully. We shall understand the deep mysteries of Providence.

[2] 1 Corinthians xv. 50.

But the knowledge, the revelation will issue in an unspeakable rapture of worship. Thus in the imagery of the *Apocalypse* it is ever worship which fills the picture of the unseen world. "The four and twenty elders fall down before Him that sat on the throne, and worship Him that liveth for ever and ever, and cast their crowns before the throne, saying, Thou art worthy, O Lord, to receive glory and honour and power ; for Thou hast created all things, and for Thy pleasure they are and were created." [1]

To sum up what has been said : The conditions of the perfected or Eternal Life in Immortality seem to be these :

1. An intuitive understanding of the Providential purpose of God as revealed in the Creation, Salvation and Regeneration of the world, but especially and pre-eminently of Mankind.
2. A loyal and happy obedience to the Will of God in ministration, self-sacrifice and purity.
3. A continuous ecstasy of devotion before the throne of God and of Christ.

These are the conditions of the heavenly life, and

[1] Revelation iv. 10, 11.

the shadow or reverse of these, with its keen, incessant sense of misery, is Hell.

But it still remains to inquire: If such is the Life Immortal, what is the relation of souls on earth to those that have passed, for happiness or woe, behind the veil? Can we do aught for them or they for us? Is intelligence possible between them and us, or sympathy or affection? The instinctive sentiment of Humanity suggests that, if the dead live after death and live a higher or more spiritual life, though it is in a sense a continuation of the present, death cannot be an absolute bar to the interests and associations which were so rich and so precious in the present life. The Christian Creed responds to this strong human sentiment by its doctrine of the Communion of Saints. It teaches that the holy ones on earth and in Heaven are knit together as members of one family by spiritual ties. Bishop Pearson, in his *Exposition of the Creed*, writes as follows:

"The communion of saints in the Church of Christ with those which are departed is demonstrated by their communion with the saints alive. For if I have a communion with a saint of God, as such, while he liveth here, I must still have communion with him when he is departed hence; because the foundation of that communion cannot be removed by death. The mystical union between Christ and His Church, the spiritual conjunction of the members to the Head, is the true foundation of that communion which one member hath with another, all the members living and increasing by the same influence which they receive from Him. But death, which is nothing else but the separation of the soul from the body, maketh no separation in the mystical union, no breach of the spiritual conjunction, and consequently there must continue the same communion, because there remaineth the same foundation." [1]

The Bishop, as is known, is singularly cautious in drawing any practical inferences from the doctrine which he expounds. Yet it would seem that the doctrine implies, if it does not actually enforce, certain lessons.

For if a sympathy exists between the living and the dead, as may be inferred not only from our Lord's explicit teaching but from the Christian conception of death itself as an entrance upon Immortality, there can be no other channel or

[1] Article ix.

instrument of such sympathy than prayer. For it is the peculiar quality of prayer that it transcends, as nothing else can, the limitations of place and time and of matter in general, and that, wherever and by whomever and for whomever it is offered, its efficacy is the same. Prayer, then, may be justly regarded as the *medium* of spiritual sympathy between the living and the dead. But the essence of prayer is mutual helpfulness. We pray for others, as they for us. We seek to strengthen them and to comfort them by our prayers. And whatever blessing we hope to receive as an answer to prayer, we are eager to give.

Christian souls, impressed with the mystery of the Universe, will be the last to doubt the helpfulness of prayer.

> "More things (says the poet) are wrought by prayer
> Than this world dreams of." [1]

And when all the mystery underlying phenomena, in the latest age of human thought as in the earliest, is deeply felt, it will be owned that opportunity remains and must remain for prayer. Intercessory prayer is the privilege of Humanity. God has not revealed its full virtue

[1] Tennyson, *The Passing of Arthur*.

or efficacy. But is it not a probable thought that the mysterious longings after holiness, the intense desires for a purity not of earth, which come we know not whence and arise we know not how in human hearts, the high immortal aspirations, are, as it were, echoes of the prayers that those who love us, as well the dead as the living, breathe for ourselves? They descend like the showers of Heaven, and like the showers they return not in vain.

But we too may and must pray for the dead, as they for us. Without such prayer the Communion of Saints becomes but a dream. We know not how or in what degree prayer is operative, although we know that so it is, upon earth, and we cannot know how it may affect them who have passed within the veil. But to pray for them is an act of faith and reverence. No act sustains so well as this the sympathy of saints. None is so potent to create and energise the assurance that the dead are still the living. None is such a witness to the reality of a purely spiritual existence and communion. None is so deep and true a solace in the presence of the realities which ever and again darken and sadden human life.

The duty or privilege of prayer for the dead does

not so much rest upon isolated passages of Holy Scripture; it rests upon the whole conception of Immortality as expressed in the Revelation of Jesus Christ. To believe in intercessory prayer for the dead is not to believe that the state of the dead is mapped out in purgatorial or other periods which a living human authority can modify at will. It is indeed the very opposite of that belief. For a belief so formal or mechanical touching the dead is opposed to the fine and sensitive outlines of the Gospel. Our Lord did not teach, nor empower any one to teach, what the future life precisely is, or how it may be affected or influenced by acts done upon earth. He taught only the doctrine of the Communion of Saints; and from that doctrine flows the spiritual sympathy, of which intercessory prayer is the expression, between the living and the dead. And he who has apprehended the eternal verity of the spiritual life will no more doubt that prayer can pass the barriers of the unseen world than he will doubt that the spirit itself passes those barriers when it is emancipated from the body at death. For Jesus Christ in His exaltation holds the keys not of Hell only (*i.e.*, of Hades), but of death.

And yet another inference seems to follow as certain. If the future life is a continuation of the present, and if prayer is the spiritual link between the visible and invisible worlds, then the helpfulness of intercessory prayer depends at once upon the possibility—I do not say the certainty—of the soul's progress or development in the future.

There is no word in Holy Scripture to suggest that the fate of souls, whether the good or the wicked, will be uniform after death. It is an assumption of a wilful Theology that all who are happy in the future Life will be equally happy, and all who suffer will suffer alike. The Scriptural intimations are wholly contrary. Our Lord speaks of some who have done wrong as being punished with many and others with few stripes. Similarly He promises that less or greater fidelity in the present life shall be rewarded with less or greater opportunity of service in the future, as in the parable of the talents, where the servant whose pound had gained ten pounds is appointed to "have authority over ten cities," and he whose pound had gained five pounds is appointed to "be over five cities."

But if a variety of destinies in the unseen world, whether of happiness or of suffering, is reserved for mankind, and yet more if the principle of that world is not inactivity but energy or character or life, it is reasonable to believe that the souls, which enter upon the future state, with the taint of sin clinging to them in whatever form or degree, will be slowly cleansed by a disciplinary or purificatory process from whatever it is that, being evil in itself, necessarily obstructs or obscures the Vision of God. The parable of Dives and Lazarus seems clearly to indicate a certain moral progress as the effect of retributory discipline. But it is natural and necessary to believe in such a progress, as a part of Christ's Revelation, if it be true, as this Essay has tended to show, that the future life is a continuation of the present, only that it is a purely spiritual life, and as such is emancipated from the limitations which render the suffering that comes of sin, as also the happiness that comes of virtue, less vivid and evident than in the nature of things they properly are. And this is the benediction of human nature, to feel that, as souls upon earth are fortified and elevated by the prayers offered for them in the unseen world, so too by our prayers may the souls which have passed behind the veil be lifted higher and higher into the knowledge and contemplation and fruition of God.

The conception of the future life, as spiritually continuing and completing the present, sheds a light upon the problem, which it is impossible to ignore, of mutual recognition in eternity. In the human hours of bereavement and desolation, when it is as though the sun had been blotted out from the heaven, we ask ourselves by the grave of our beloved ones, Shall we meet again ? Shall we know one another in Heaven ? To this deep anxiety of the heart Shakespeare gives expression in the lines where Constance cries—

> " Father cardinal, I have heard you say
> That we shall see and know our friends in heaven :
> If that be true, I shall see my boy again ;
> For since the birth of Cain, the first male child
> To him that did but yesterday suspire,
> There was not such a gracious creature born.
> But now will canker sorrow eat my bud,
> And chase the native beauty from his cheek,
> And he will look as hollow as a ghost ;
> As dim and meagre as an ague's fit ;
> And so he'll die ; and, rising so again,
> When I shall meet him in the court of heaven,
> I shall not know him : therefore never, never
> Must I behold my pretty Arthur more." [1]

---

[1] *King John*, Act iii. scene iv.

Nor is any satisfaction of this anxiety possible, unless it be found in the Revelation of Jesus Christ. But if the spiritual life of Man be, as He taught, eternal, and if it be a life beginning on earth but transcending the earthly bounds of place or time, then the identity of the life before and after death would seem to imply that they who knew and loved each other upon earth will not forfeit the exquisite happiness of such mutual knowledge and love in the world to come. For that which passes into Immortality is the whole man, except only his body. It is the person himself, his consciousness, his intellect, his moral, emotional and spiritual being. For personality survives death. It is the soul, which begins a new or larger life, but does not begin life, behind the veil. The earthly human material relations of the present life disappear when the body moulders in the grave, as our Lord Himself teaches when He says that there is no such thing as marrying or giving in marriage in eternity; but the spiritual affections and affinities endure eternally. And, where no loss of personality takes place, the power of mutual recognition must remain.

The poet of the *In Memoriam* in his musings upon the Eternal Life in which he exhibited so strong a faith puts this truth clearly—

> "Eternal form shall still divide
> The eternal soul from all beside;
> And I shall know him when we meet."

Such is the Christian thought of the dead as living still, and living a life more subtle and spiritual than upon earth; and of all thoughts it is perhaps the most hallowing, the most ennobling in its influence upon mankind. For he who believes in the life of the dead must himself live not unworthily of the dead.

> "How pure at heart and sound in head,
> With what Divine affections bold
> Should be the man whose thought would hold
> An hour's communion with the dead."

Le culte des morts—that beautiful habit and act of the Catholic Faith—needs revival in Protestant Theology. Protestantism, which so well exhibits the strength, and so ill the poetry or romance of religion, and is always in danger of losing the delicate flower of devotion, has too much forgotten the dead. It has buried them out of mind as out of sight. It has not thought of them as dwelling in communion with the progress, the sympathies, the aspirations of the holy and eternal souls upon earth. It will not be altogether in vain that this Essay has been written, if it shall help to inspire any living human soul with a more tender and constant memory of the dead. The Festival of All Souls is a commemoration which enriches and ennobles Humanity.

Thus to one who lives on earth the Eternal Life which is Christ's revelation and benediction to the world, death, it would seem, makes some such difference as this : It is a rending of the veil of the flesh. It is a passing, as it were, within the sanctuary. It is a quickening of the intellectual and moral sensibility. The faculties and energies of the soul are intensified, as the material barriers which the body sets to them are done away. Thus faith merges in knowledge. Hope attains to realisation. Life becomes a pure spiritual activity. Whatever is gross or material or sensual in human nature ceases. Whatever is pure and sacred is purified and sanctified. The soul, unclouded and unimpeded, stands before God. This is the celestial state ; the beatific vision. It is for this that the saints have prayed so long and striven. Of its felicity they have enjoyed glimpses few and far, as when St. Paul was " caught up to the third heaven " and " heard unspeakable words which it is not lawful for a man to utter."[1] But such rapture is only the faint anticipation of the

[1] 2 Corinthians xii. 24.

beatitude which the souls, redeemed by Christ, enjoy for ever and ever.

Of Hell, as it is called, and of the disciplinary process to which unhallowed souls are subjected when this life is ended, it is impossible to form a conception save through the contrast in which it stands to the beatific state; for it has not been the Will of God to reveal more than its mere shadowy outline. But if the flesh or material part of human nature is indeed, as has been argued in this essay, a force that mitigates and obscures the natural necessary effect of the Divine indignation against sin, it must be inferred that, when the soul stands at the Judgment-bar, the misery of sin, the pain of loss, the burning sense of all that might have been and yet is not and may never be, above all the ever present consciousness of alienation from Him to Whom Man's spiritual being tends unceasingly, will be an agony so sharp and subtle as to extort an exceeding bitter cry for the pardon and peace of Heaven. Beyond this point Revelation does not pass; and it were idle, if not even impious, to dream of passing. God has taught in His Gospel as much as Man needs to know for his conduct in life; it has not been the Divine Will to teach more.

AMPLIFICATION OF THE BELIEF

But the Christian Revelation adds to the creed of Immortality one special doctrine which may not be omitted, though it may be felt to lie beyond the just scope of this Essay. It is the doctrine of the corporeal Resurrection. It demands consideration, because at first sight it seems to make against the pure and perfect spirituality of the Life Immortal.

And, indeed, it is a doctrine which must be accepted, if at all, upon the authority of a Divine Revelation. It is not recommended by such general arguments as have been adduced in behalf of Immortality. The analogies of which Nature is full, though persuasively used by a thinker so profound as St. Paul, must be admitted, as has been urged in the fourth chapter of this Essay, to possess but slight evidential validity as witnesses to the corporeal resurrection of the dead.

It is not in this way that the Resurrection has been taught to the world. It is a belief distinctively Christian. The Apostles of Christianity believed, and insisted upon belief in the Resurrection, because they believed that Jesus Christ had risen from the grave.

Of the evidence for the Resurrection this is not

the place to speak. All that need be said is that His Resurrection must not be treated as if it were the final act of a Life which was in all respects, except this act, assimilated to the common conditions of Humanity. The Resurrection was not an extraordinary event in an ordinary life; it was the extraordinary consummation of a Life which, from its beginning to its end, was all extraordinary. That Jesus Christ should rise from the grave was undoubtedly a superhuman event. But His claims to be sinless, to forgive the sins of others, to be the Judge of the quick and the dead, were equally superhuman. It is the whole Life—the whole Personality —of Jesus Christ, not His Resurrection alone, which stands upon a higher than human level of being. His whole Life, His whole Personality is superhuman; but it is uniform.

To Christian hearts the Resurrection of Jesus Christ is an absolute assurance that the dead shall rise. "If the dead rise not, then is not Christ raised: and if Christ be not raised, your faith is vain; ye are yet in your sins."[1] For by His Resurrection—the most completely attested event in the origin of Christianity—He proved for all time that, where the

[1] 1 Corinthians xv. 16, 17.

Spirit is supreme in human nature, death, as an ultimate fact, is impossible; and in proportion as men are inheritors of His Nature, His Immortality is theirs; and the Resurrection of His body is an evidence, as it is an illustration, of the destiny awaiting theirs beyond the grave. His Resurrection, then, is a proof of Immortality; for it could not be true if Immortality were not a truth.

But while the Resurrection of Jesus Christ, involving, as it seems, the Resurrection of Mankind, is always treated in the *Acts of the Apostles* and in the Epistles as the very heart of the Christian Revelation, it would not be consistent with the purpose of this Essay to go beyond the question, What will be the nature of the body as it rises into life? The New Testament supplies an answer to that question so far as it affects the bodies of the holy dead, but not otherwise. For in the New Testament two distinct Resurrections are contemplated—the general resurrection of all men, called in the Greek ἡ ἀνάστασις τῶν νεκρῶν, and the special resurrection of Christians, called ἡ ἐξανάστασις ἡ ἐκ τῶν νεκρῶν, though it is true that some variety of terms occurs. It is to the specially Christian Resurrection that I now refer.

There are, then, in Christian Theology, two bodies, or phases of the same body, belonging to every man.

One is "the body of humiliation," *i.e.*, the body which he possesses upon earth, a weak, fragile, material, perishing, sinful body.

The other is "the body of glory," *i.e.*, the same body but no longer material or moribund, a body conformable to the body which our Lord Himself possesses in His glory.[1]

And the change which will pass upon the human body at the Resurrection is that it will emerge, as the butterfly from the chrysalis, out of its present material environment into a purified and glorified existence.

Bishop Pearson hardly rises to an adequate realisation of the celestial body in its dignity and spirituality when he writes, "We can, therefore, no otherwise expound this article, touching 'the resurrection of the body,' than by asserting that the bodies which have lived and died shall live again after death, and that the same flesh which is corrupted shall be restored ; whatsoever alteration shall be made shall not be of their nature, but of

[1] See Philippians iii. 21.

their conditions ; not of their substance, but of their qualities." [1]

The body at its Resurrection will be the same body, but it will be glorified. It will be emancipated from the limiting and tainting conditions of matter. It will be a spiritual and sacred body. It will be such a body as is necessary to personality, but not such as is necessary to material life.

What the body will then be it is not given to Man to realise, unless approximately and figuratively. But there is one incident of the Gospel which illustrates its nature. It is told that our Lord on one occasion " took Peter and John and James, and went up into a mountain to pray. And as He prayed the fashion of His countenance was altered and His raiment was white and glistering. And behold, there talked with Him two men, which were Moses and Elias ; who appeared in glory, and spake of His decease which He should accomplish at Jerusalem." [2]

The Transfiguration—that unique event in His human history—exemplifies the change which shall pass upon the body at its Resurrection. It indicates that the glory of the Lord shall be shared by His

[1] *Exposition of the Creed.* Article xi.   [2] Luke ix. 28-31.

saints; for Moses and Elias appeared with Him "in glory." It indicates, too, the possibility of a spiritual communion far transcending the limits of time or place or condition; for the three disciples knew and recognised the saints of olden days; and so it sheds a light upon the life of Heaven.

The Resurrection of the body is, as has been said, a Christian doctrine. It is believed, simply and solely, on the authority of the Lord and His Apostles. But it completes or consummates the theory of Redemption as sanctifying the whole triune nature of Man. It places the body in its true light, not as a mere prison-house of the spirit, not as a necessary centre and source of evil, but as a material form endued with a sovereign destiny, or, in St. Paul's words, as "a shrine of the Holy Spirit."

But all that need here be said is that in this true conception of the body of the Resurrection there is nothing that militates against the pure, immortal, spiritual, eternal life for which this Essay has been a plea. For this is certain that, when the body revives at the Resurrection, it will not be a material body, but etherealised and glorified. The faith of Christ adds a glorified, immortal body, however it may be most justly imagined, to a glorified, immortal soul.

This is the full doctrine of Immortality as revealed in the Gospel.

Immortality, as this Essay has argued, is the inalienable prerogative of Man. It is the prerogative not of his body but of his soul and, above all, of his spirit. At death the human body is dissolved ; but the soul survives in the plenitude of its intellectual, moral and spiritual powers.

Jesus Christ revealed "the Eternal Life," which was His own Life, as the true or perfect life of the soul. And they in whom "the Eternal Life" is realised possess in themselves the secret of Immortality. To attain this Life is the hope and effort of Christians. To give it to others was the privilege of Christ. Human nature, in winning "the Eternal Life" has reached the highest point of which it is or can ever be capable. It is the life that the angels live. In the cloudless contemplation of God's glory, in the luminous understanding of His Providence, in the devout adoration of His wisdom and His love, the human soul, being emancipated from the bonds of the material body, enjoys and exhibits its full affinity to the Godhead.

Beyond and above human apprehension lies "the Eternal Life" in its integrity. It is begun, it is not completed or perfected, on earth. No living soul may know its wonders or its joys. To it belong the things that eye has never seen, nor ear heard, nor heart conceived. It is the fruition of peace and purity and love. It is the satisfaction of the longings and desires by which human nature on earth is quickened and sanctified.

All that is vital to Humanity depends upon the faith of the soul's Immortality. To plead for that faith, to make it reasonable and acceptable, has been the object of this Essay. For to Man it is all in all. Without it life is poor and sad and purposeless. It were better—I speak as I think—not to be born. But the soul which looks to the infinite spaces of Immortality may wait, in tranquil hope and faith, until God shall in His mercy make the mysteries of life to be clear. For where the Eternal Life springs up in the soul, there is the peace that passes understanding.

May they who read this Essay—and he too who has written it—not come short of "the Eternal Life," which is in Christ Jesus!

RECENTLY PUBLISHED.

THE LIFE AND WORK OF CHARLES PRITCHARD,
D.D., F.R.S., late Savilian Professor of Astronomy in the University of Oxford. Memoirs compiled by his Daughter, ADA PRITCHARD, with an Account of his Theological Work by the Bishop of WORCESTER. and of his Astronomical Work by Professor H. H. TURNER, F.R.A.S, With a Portrait. Demy 8vo, cloth, 10s. 6d.

"It is hardly too much to say that had Pritchard's lot been cast in a more public sphere his influence on education might scarcely have been second to that of Arnold himself. So much we may judge from the emphatic testimony borne in these memoirs to the originality of his methods and the brilliancy of their results by such high authorities as the Dean of Westminster, Sir George Grove, Sir William Herschel, and other distinguished men, who were his pupils. ... The memoirs are full of interest from the personal point of view ... the portrait of a very remarkable personality."—*Times.*

SIERRA LEONE AFTER A HUNDRED YEARS.
By the Right Rev. E. G. INGHAM, late Bishop of Sierra Leone. With Sixteen Illustrations. Large crown 8vo, cloth, 6s.

"Not for many a day have we read anything so wise and straightforward on the conversion of the heathen as the latter part of Bishop Ingham's singularly interesting book."—*Daily News.*

NEW CHINA AND OLD : Notes on the Country and
the People, made during a Residence of Thirty Years. Second Edition. By Ven. ARTHUR E. MOULE, Archdeacon of Ningpo, and C.M.S. Missionary. With Thirty Illustrations. Cloth, 7s. 6d.

"This book ministers to hopefulness. It has set out with great interest, and expressed with much minuteness, the peculiar spiritual necessities of the Chinese mind."—*Record.*

THE ARAB AND THE AFRICAN. By S. T. PRUEN,
M.D., F.R.G.S. With Illustrations. Cloth, 6s.

"A more sensible, unaffected account of the country and its people has not come before us for a long time."—*Daily Chronicle.*

JAMES HANNINGTON, FIRST BISHOP OF
EASTERN EQUATORIAL AFRICA. A History of his Life and Work. By the Rev. E. C. DAWSON, M.A. Thirty-fifth Thousand. Price 3s. 6d. cloth, or 2s. 6d. paper boards.

"We doubt whether a nobler or more pathetic story has ever been told in biography."—*Athenæum.*

LONDON: SEELEY & CO. LIMITED, 38, GREAT RUSSELL STREET.

THEOLOGICAL BOOKS.

THE SACRIFICE OF CHRIST: Its Vital Reality and Efficacy. By the Rev. HENRY WACE, D.D., Prebendary of St. Paul's, and Examining Chaplain to the Archbishop of Canterbury. Fcap. 8vo, cloth, 1s.

OUR PRAYER BOOK. Short Chapters on the History and Contents of the Book of Common Prayer. By the Rev. H. C. G. MOULE, D.D., Principal of Ridley Hall, Cambridge. 16mo, cloth, 1s.

THE CROSS AND THE SPIRIT. Studies in the Epistles to the Galatians. By the Rev. H. C. G. MOULE, D.D. 1s. 6d.

GRACE AND GODLINESS. Studies in the Epistle to the Ephesians. By the Rev. H. C. G. MOULE, D.D. Cloth, 2s. 6d.

JESUS AND THE RESURRECTION. Expository Chapters on St. John xx. and xxi. By the Rev. H. C. G. MOULE, D.D. Second Edition. Cloth, 2s. 6d.

BISHOP RIDLEY ON THE LORD'S SUPPER. A Brief Declaration of the Lord's Supper, written by NICHOLAS RIDLEY, Bishop of London. Reprinted with Introductions, Notes, and Appendices, and Prefaced by a Life of the Writer, by the Rev. H. C. G. MOULE, D.D. With Illustrations. Crown 8vo, cloth, 5s.

AT THE HOLY COMMUNION. Helps for Preparation and Reception. By the Rev. H. C. G. MOULE, D.D. Twentieth Thousand. Cloth, 1s.

SECRET PRAYER. By the Rev. H. C. G. MOULE, D.D. Twenty-fifth Thousand. Cloth, 1s.

BAPTISM—WHAT SAITH THE SCRIPTURE? By the Rev. DAVID H. D. WILKINSON. With a Preface by the Rev. H. C. G. MOULE, D.D. Second Edition. Cloth, 1s. 6d.

ON SERMON PREPARATION: Recollections and Suggestions. By the BISHOP OF RIPON, the DEAN OF NORWICH, the DEAN OF CANTERBURY, ARCHDEACON SINCLAIR, CANON TRISTRAM, PREBENDARY WEBB PEPLOE, Rev. H. C. G. MOULE, D.D., Rev. F. J. CHAVASSE, Rev. W. H. M. H. AITKEN, Rev. A. J. HARRISON, D.D., Rev. H. SUTTON, and Rev. A. R. BUCKLAND. 3s. 6d.

LONDON: SEELEY & CO. LIMITED, 38, GREAT RUSSELL STREET.

www.ingramcontent.com/pod-product-compliance
Lightning Source LLC
Chambersburg PA
CBHW021240240426
43673CB00057B/916